COUNTRY ROOTS

COUNTRY ROOTS
The Origins of Country Music

DOUGLAS B. GREEN
Foreword by Merle Travis

Hawthorn Books, Inc.
Publishers / NEW YORK

SONG TITLE CREDITS
(As used in chapter titles)

"Carry Me Back to the Mountains," by Carson J. Robison, © 1930, 1956 by Peer International. "Everybody's Had the Blues," by Merle Haggard, © 1973 by Shade Tree Music. "Back in the Saddle Again," by Ray Whitley and Gene Autry, © 1939, 1956, by Western Music. "Big Mamou," by Link Davis © 1953 by Peer International. "Blue Moon of Kentucky" by Bill Monroe, © 1947, 1975 by Peer International. "Home in San Antone," by Fred Rose, © 1943 by Milene Music. "Blue Suede Shoes," by Carl Perkins, © 1955 by Hilo/Hill & Range. "Bright Lights and Country Music," by Bill Anderson and Jimmy Gately, © 1965 by Moss Rose Publications.

COUNTRY ROOTS

 All inquiries should be addressed to Hawthorn Books, Inc., 260 Madison Avenue, New York, New York 10016. This book was manufactured in the United States of America and published simultaneously in Canada by Prentice-Hall of Canada, Limited, 1870 Birchmount Road, Scarborough, Ontario.

Library of Congress Catalog Card Number: 75-28691

ISBN: hardcover, 0-8015-1781-8; softcover, 0-8015-1778-8

1 2 3 4 5 6 7 8 9 10

For Liza Jane and Sally Anne;
it is by them the sun rises and sets.

CONTENTS

FOREWORD
by Merle Travis

Country music, rich in history and even more abundant in roots, is many things to many people. And this well-written book captures that wealth—not an easy task. My friend Doug Green tells us that his book is not a scholarly history but an interpretive look at the history of country music. Unfortunately, written pages cannot be for any reader the entire country music experience. In order to taste that encounter, according to Doug, one would have to spend "years upon years listening to radio . . . seeing live shows, reading a thousand . . . fan and scholarly articles and magazines, and buying thousands of dollars' worth of records." Well, in my nearly forty years as a country musician, with the exception of spending a small fortune, I have done it all. And so, while this book might be for many readers a words-and-pictures shortcut to the country music experience, for me it is my own scrapbook. I know most of the artists mentioned and feel proud of them—they are truly roots of the great country music tree.

In all honesty, I must admit that a history of country music, or even an interpretation of it, can never replace my own accumulation of memories. My own record collection, much of it on cylinders, contains what we call country music but actually dates back to shortly after the turn of the century. (My copy of the Sears Roebuck 1908 catalog advertises Columbia cylinder records at 18 cents each or $2.15 per dozen!) I own an Edison "talking machine" in perfect playing condition—a gift from my dear friend Hank Thompson, the leader of a western swing band that was named by the trade magazines the best western swing band thirteen years in a row. And I remember artists such as Henry Burr, Collin and Harlan, Ada Jones, and Cal Stewart (as "Uncle Josh"), who became wealthy by selling millions of cylinders long before Vernon Dalhart's classic "Prisoner Song" sold a million records—years after the old cylinder talking machine went to its final resting place in some dusty attic. I got my information from the chairman of the board of Sears Roebuck & Company and one of the grandest men I know, "Uncle" Art Satherly, who actually worked with Thomas A. Edison.

Still, Doug Green's book does work to cover almost every aspect of country music. I feel fortunate—if not almost like a relic—to have performed within each one of these phases in my forty years as a country entertainer. And if I didn't actually play the music, at least, as Irving S. Cobb would say, "I stood on the sidelines and cheered."

The old-time music experience was an especially sentimental one. In the early days of radio I saw tears roll down the cheeks of my friend Red Foley as he sang of "Mother's Old Red Shawl." As for the blues, I grew up listening to the black men in my Muhlenberg County home in Kentucky sing such lyrics as:

Jelly roll, jelly roll,
It ain't hard to find,
Run my Gran'pa crazy,
Run my Gran'ma blind.
They love the jelly roll,
Sweet jelly roll,
Once you taste that jelly
Yo' mama can't keep you home. . . .

And then there's the country comedian with his red wig, oversized trousers, a blackened tooth, and of course, the straight man. In a typical routine the comic would tell of his girlfriend named Bureau. The straight man would protest, "But a bureau is about this high and about this wide and has great long drawers." "That's her!" the comic would quip. Corny? For sure. But often, before the show got underway, audiences would request, "Be sure to pull that one about the bureau."

Doug covers the western cowboys quite well, although I might be inclined to disagree with him when he says that all the western has gone out of country. Just a few nights before this writing Marty Robins and his trio sang three beautiful western songs on a national TV broadcast celebrating the fiftieth anniversary of the Grand Ole Opry. All three were written by that genius bard Bob Nolan, who wrote such everlasting pieces of music like "Cool Water" and "Tumbling Tumbleweeds" and hundreds more. Now that's what I call western.

And travel across the bayou country of Louisiana, as I hope many of you have, and you'll hear on your radio songs in French and broken English, often accompanied by an accordion and fiddle, played as only the fun-loving Cajuns can play. It's a flavorful, distinct sound, and through it the bayou country will live forever.

Then, of course, there's bluegrass music, which actually got its name from Bill Monroe, a Kentuckian. After Bill and his brother Charlie went their separate ways, Bill called his band the Blue Grass Boys after his home state. (Bill is from Rosine, in Ohio County, which is the next door neighbor to my home county, Muhlenberg.) Other bands, picking up on Bill's sound, started calling their music bluegrass too, even though some of them were from Vermont and Utah, where bluegrass doesn't grow at all. Anyway, although the music is still growing and changing today, you're still apt to hear old favorites like "Rollin' in My Sweet Baby's Arms," "Blue Moon of Kentucky," and "Salty Dog."

The country music panorama goes on and on. The dance-hall bands in the Southwest with their fiddles, electric steel guitars, and very often wind instruments, raised the roof with such songs as "Stay All Night, Stay a Little Longer," "Take Me Back to Tulsa," and "San Antino Rose." At the opposite end of the spectrum are gospel songs and hymns. They're actually cousins, but there's a big difference between the rollicking gospel song "I'll Fly Away," which is a spirited piece of music akin to the style of Monroe's Blue Grass Boys, and the sweet spiritual standard, "Swing Low, Sweet Chariot" or the somber hymn "The Old Rugged Cross." Then in the 1950s the youngsters came up with a dozen different kinds of music all rolled into one and gave it a number of names—rockabilly, country rock, and rock and roll among them. If you ask me, they're not much more than the black man's twelve-bar blues sung at a highly spirited pace, actually a cousin to boogie-woogie and the spiritual.

Finally there's the Nashville sound—songs ground out by professional song writers, sung by skilled singers, accompanied by highly professional musicians. It's music based on a tell-it-like-it-is altitude and recorded on the latest and most sophisticated sound equipment. It gave rise to songs like "Behind Closed Doors" and "Help Me Make It Through the Night." This last sentiment is a long way from "tears gleaming like gems on mother's old red shawl." But so it goes. . . .

And that seems to bring us to the last page of the scrapbook. It's a rich story, for sure, and one that conjures up in my mind endless images of a musical tradition in which I am proud to have taken part. *Country Roots* is a loving tribute to a music that deserves just that.

Merle Travis

ACKNOWLEDGMENTS

Of the many people who have contributed substantially in my behalf, I would especially like to single out Jim McGuire, not only for his many superb photographs but for bringing the possiblility of this book to my attention.

In addition, my sincere thanks go to Bill Ivey and Bob Pinson of the Country Music Foundation for their tireless help in correcting, criticizing, and reviewing the manuscript; and to Danny Hatcher and the staff at the Library and Media Center of the Country Music Foundation for assistance and guidance in the archives.

To J. Clark Thomas for his photo reproductions thanks are also due; and special thanks to Sandra Choron, who coaxed and counseled me through troubled times to make this book possible. A better editor one couldn't hope to have.

And for inspiration I must, of course, thank my wise, gentle, but sometimes balky muse, Clio.

COUNTRY ROOTS

LOOK WHO'S COMING

UNCLE DAVE MACON

AND

SAM McGEE

BOTH FROM TENNESSEE

VOCALION RECORD ARTISTS

You are getting yourself TOLD about something entertaining and Worth While by seeing them in person. THEY DO DOUBLES AND SINGLES WITH BANJO AND GUITAR, INSTRUMENTAL AND VOCAL.

Uncle Dave Macon is the only man in captivity who plays and sings on two banjos at the same time. TRICK BANJO PLAYING IS HIS SPECIALTY.

Funny, Clean Jokes and Lots of Fun
BRING THE WHOLE FAMILY
WILL APPEAR HERE

High School — La Fayette

Friday Aug 31 8 P.M.

ADMISSION 15 & 25 ¢

I
INTRODUCTION
"Gifts from over the Sea"

Country music: the name means so much and so little. It is as specific for one person as it is vague for another, covering too much territory for some and not enough for others. Some see it as the hard-living songs of a hard-living people, some as the cry of a socially and financially oppressed minority, others as the voice of a strong but silent majority, and still others as the soul of a land and a region. It is all these and much more: It is a giant and—until recently—often neglected tree whose roots into the fertile ground of time and tradition and culture are long and deep and whose branches are many, spreading out broadly to cover a great deal of ground.

This book is not a scholarly history: Bill C. Malone has already written that in his excellent *Country Music USA: A Fifty Year History*. It is not an encyclopedia: There are already three of those listed in the Bibliography. And it is also not a history of the business side of country music, a side that, although few entertainers, musicians, scholars, or fans care to admit it, has changed and affected the history of country music every bit as much as those whose names we see on the finished product, the record labels. That fascinating book has yet to be written.

What this book is, then, more than anything, is an interpretive look at the history of country music, one that will impart both knowledge and, it is hoped, a little insight to the expert and devoted fan and give a sense of perspective to the neophyte who sees strange, evocative words like *Cajun, down-home gospel,* and *bluegrass* splashed indiscriminately across record jackets and cropping up again and again in liner notes. It should give those who are familiar with the history of the music a few different angles on it, and to those who aren't, it should provide, in brief, an understanding that otherwise could only be obtained by spending years upon years listening to radio (in all regions of America), seeing live shows, reading the articles in *Country Song Roundup* and a thousand other fan and scholarly magazines, and buying thousands of dollars' worth of records. It is a short cut, in words and in pictures, that will cover over fifty years of recorded history (and hundreds of years of oral tradition) to furnish a perspective on what has happened and, at least in one opinion, why. An interpretive look at the history of the origins of country music—that seems to sum it up as well as anything.

The name itself: country music. Music from, by, about the people of the American countryside. It seems so simple, yet the name endured several complicated evolutions. First it was old-time tunes. And when an A&R man (for Artist and Repertoire, one who runs a recording session and is responsible for matching the entertainers signed by his label with many of the tunes recorded) named Ralph Peer asked a young fiddler named Al Hopkins what he called his band, the reply was, "Call the band anything you want. We're just a bunch of hillbillies from North Carolina and Virginia, anyway." His band then became known as the Hillbillies, and the record industry, picking up the cue, began calling it hillbilly music.

Hillbilly was almost always distasteful to the performers and musicians, who craved a deeper national understanding and certainly greater respect for their music and the music business. *Billboard,* one of the industry's major magazines carrying the "charts" as well as industry news items, flirted briefly with *folk*—for southeastern music—and *hot dance*—for western swing before encompassing it all under the term *country and western,* which soon was abbreviated to C&W. The idea, apparently, was to give the dignity of the success (financial, that is) of the singing

RECREATION HALL
IN CITY PARK
STEPHENVILLE, TEXAS

THURSDAY, DEC. 11th   8:00 P. M.

STARS *of* STAGE, SCREEN, RADIO

IN PERSON

DWIGHT BUTCHER'S

WBAP - KGKO

RADIO JAMBOREE

—FEATURING—

THE CHUCK WAGON GANG
CEDAR RIDGE BOYS
ERNEST TUBB (*Recording Artist*)
CECIL BROWER   FAY SMITH
CARTER QUARTETTE
RED WOODWARD   DWIGHT BUTCHER
AND OTHERS

Admission   ADULTS: - - 40c, Tax 4c
      CHILDREN: - 20c, Tax 2c

Sponsored by
THE AMERICAN LEGION
of Stephenville

cowboy to what had been called hillbilly music, hoping, somehow, to legitimize what many considered a strange and irritating phenomenon. But after some time, it became apparent that country and western was a somewhat illogical pairing (much like saying "country and Cajun" or "country and bluegrass", that country music was a large, healthy tree that encompassed western or cowboy music as one of its many subgenres. And so the "and western" was dropped (although, unfortunately, not by some of the national media to this day) in favor of the more accurate "country," which it is now called with relative comfort by industry, fan, and entertainer alike. There was a move afoot not long ago to call it "American music," but the blatant unfairness to other equally deserving American musical forms was apparently obvious to most of those who heard the new phrase, and the expression never caught on. So it has been country music for well over a decade now, and it seems likely to remain that way for a while at least.

The evolution of the name is easier to describe than the evolution of the music itself, for it is basically an ancient music, rooted in a heady mixture of cultures and peoples. The following chapters sketch the roots (and the branches) that have shaped and affected this music, but there is a deep main root (can the analogy be extended to call it a taproot?) as well as several slender roots that are too small to warrant chapters in and of themselves, but that nonetheless have had a profound influence on the growth and development of this magnificent and outstretched tree we call country music.

Entertainment in rural England, Scotland, and Ireland was rare and highly prized hundreds of years ago. In a place and a time where there was little to relieve the drudgery of working the land, the chief means of entertainment was the telling, in song, of long narrative stories of love, adventure, history, and the supernatural. These stories, these ballads, handed down from one generation to the next, some-times intact, sometimes remembered imperfectly or fragmentarily, represent the taproot of the tree of country music. Rhythmless, sung in a high, mournful, stiff-jawed style, they would be barely listenable to our modern ears, but they were for the people of medieval Britain (and for the populations in isolated pockets of both the New and Old Worlds almost up to the present) what country music is for us today: entertainment, release, escape in tales of romantic history and adventure, and heartfelt expressions of sorrow, grief, and love. The performance was un-polished by our standards, but the effect—and that is the heart of every musical form—was much the same: It moved those people to tears and to fright and to laughter, just as country music does today.

Instrumentalists were much scarcer than singers in those far-off days. When, over two thousand years ago, the Anglo-Saxons drove the Celts into the hinterlands that were to become Scotland and Ireland, the retreating peoples took with them their bagpipes, the musical traces of which can still be heard in a droning fiddle break or a lonesome, modal banjo tune. (In fact, Glen Campbell played his own bagpipes on his recent hit recording of "Bonaparte's Retreat.") But bagpipe players were few and far between (remnants of the bagpipe can be found in the sound of the mountain dulcimer, a scarce but haunting instrument), and while instrumental talent existed,

The Ryman Auditorium, home of the Grand Ole Opry for nearly thirty years. Often referred to as the mother church of country music, the Ryman was actually the fifth home to which the cast of the Opry moved. They are now comfortably ensconced in an ultra-plush new auditorium on the grounds of Opryland U.S.A. (*Grease Brothers*)

the instruments did not. In about 1550 the violin as we know it was developed, and thereafter spread northward from its native Italy with suprising speed. Soon the peoples of the relatively remote British Isles began to feel a great kinship toward this instrument, which could be made to sound so much like a bagpipe, and here, really, instrumental accompaniment was born in the distant past of what was to become country music.

A fiddle was small, light, and, although fragile, easily carried, and to the musically oriented, it was the handiest of available (and versatile) instruments to take aboard ship when crossing the rough Atlantic to that new land of unlimited opportunities and endless forests called America. Fiddles came over with the earliest settlers and became a firm part of American folk tradition, both in the Northeast (as well as Canada) and in the South.

The mountain dulcimer, a rare and beautiful instrument that combines the tone of a wooden instrument with the tuning and feel of bagpipes. It is held here by Jean Ritchie, of Viper, Kentucky, who made the instrument famous in folk-music circles in the 1950s and 1960s. (*Country Music Foundation Library and Media Center*)

In fact, in American folk tradition, fiddle music or instrumental music is much more common than vocal; many performers echo Roy Acuff's statement that he and his contemporary musicians rarely thought of singing a song outside of church and that their main musical focus was the entertainment of themselves as musicians (not singers) and of their friends and neighbors as dancers. If much of country music history seems, at first glance, heavily weighted with the excess baggage of types of instruments and styles of playing, it is because of the traditional preoccupation with instrumental music that has characterized country music down through the years. There was, however, a very definite relationship between early instrumentals and their singing counterparts, who did little more than imitate their fiddle accompaniment note for note. Only with commercial pressure to change did singing and fiddling go their separate ways.

America's explosive expansion after the War of Independence left pockets of culture high and dry, particularly in the rugged and inhospitable Appalachians, virtually untouched by passing centuries until the turn of this century, when "progress," in the mixed blessing of railroads and coal mines, came to the isolated dales and hollows of the mountains of Kentucky, Tennessee, Virginia, West Virginia, and Georgia. Here the isolated mountaineer, who played the same fiddle tunes and sang the same ballads as his or her great-great-grandparents, was suddenly confronted with the black section worker, who laid track throughout the southern highlands and brought with him another small, portable instrument called the guitar, which was perfect for the accompaniment of singing—far better than the high-pitched, scratchy, lonesome fiddle.

Jamming at the Opry. (*Grease Brothers*)

The guitar wasn't entirely unknown in the South (or in other parts of America) before the turn of the century. Andrew Jackson's daughter-in-law bought one as early as 1819 which can still be seen at The Hermitage, Jackson's estate just outside of Nashville, and in 1833 C. F. Martin found enough of a market to justify building his famous guitars. But in those early days the guitar was considered a refined instrument for proper young ladies to study and perform in the parlor. In fact, several "popular" tunes of Jackson's day, "Fisher's Hornpipe" for example, have filtered down into tradition, musicians thinking of them now as old fiddle tunes. Even the old fiddle warhorse "The Eighth of January" was, of course, written to commemorate Jackson's victory at New Orleans during the War of 1812.

Despite its early use, the guitar had little impact on the rocky, isolated pockets of medieval culture hidden away in the deep Appalachians until the coming of the black section workers, who brought with their guitars an African-based musical style that emphasized rhythm, always severely lacking in Anglo-Celtic musical tradition. It is interesting in this regard to listen to traditional Irish records, both foreign and American-Irish, because the vocal style—accent aside—is pure country music, and the haunting melodies are the very heart of most of this music. And even the instruments—fiddle and concertina, sometimes guitar—are well within country music tradition; but there is no rhythm: The singer sings a phrase, pauses, sings another, pauses, and sings yet another. It took the solid, steady rhythm of the black guitarists as taught to white children to move country music away from the ballad tradition and add to it a sound and a feel that partially characterizes it today.

Meanwhile, in the barren Southwest and Far West, a similar set of circumstances existed, for there the settlers who had left Virginia and Tennessee to settle the Great Plains were picking up the guitar from the Spanish vaqueros south of the border, finding the instrument, once again, easily carried, easily played, and a perfect accompaniment to their cattle calls on lonely prairie nights, adding a certain south-of-the-border flavor to the haunting Irish tunes they traditionally sang. It is particularly interesting that some of that flavor is returning to recent country music, with the blossoming of such bilingual singers as Johnny Rodriguez and Freddy Fender.

With the spread of the minstrel show in pre- and post-Civil War America came the popularity of the banjo, an instrument of African descent. The sound of the five-string banjo (supposedly invented by a Joe Sweeney in the 1830s), with its high drone string, and the fact that it could easily be tuned to play in lonesome-sounding modes made it a favorite instrument among mountain musicians. As Lester Flatt is fond of recounting, many a "band" in the early days consisted of nothing but a fiddle and a banjo, usually played in a style alternately called frailing, drop-thumb, or clawhammer—which involved ringing the fifth, or drone, string with the thumb and brushing the other strings with the fingers—a style that could be both delicate and rambunctious. Occasionally a banjoist would play in a two-finger style (actually thumb and finger), more reminiscent of today's familiar bluegrass style, but still far from the degree of complexity that Earl Scruggs introduced to the instrument. Early recording artists like Dock Boggs achieved marvelous effects with this instrument, using its lonesome hollow sound and eerie modal tunings to highlight spectral songs like "Oh Death."

Then, too, with the opening of exotic foreign lands to American trade shortly before the turn of the century, a marked faddishness for the unusual overtook

American culture in general; merely note the number of Japanese-style houses built between 1900 and 1910. There was also a surge of interest in things Mediterranean, perhaps due in part to the great wave of immigrants from southern Europe shortly before the turn of the century. And it was in this manner that the mandolin was introduced, first to classically oriented music but eventually filtering into the mountains. A furniture-maker in Kalamazoo, Michigan, named Orville Gibson adapted the gourd-shaped Italian mandolin to modern playing, making it flatter

(more like a guitar or violin) and lengthening the scale, which made for a far better-sounding and better-playing instrument. Thus the mandolin—especially the Gibson brand— became extremely popular in a wide variety of musical circumstances: mandolin orchestras, vaudeville, and eventually among the mountain people of the highland South.

Another fad that was to have an enormous effect on country music was the interest in the Hawaiian Islands, which came under U.S. control in 1898. The haunting music of these islands, which, like most Polynesian music, is surprisingly but extremely Western in tone, scale, and harmony (as opposed to music of the Asian continent) became an immediate success stateside. It didn't take long before the sounds of the ukulele and the Hawaiian guitar (a standard guitar laid flat across the lap and played with a steel bar in the left hand which slid across the strings rather than fretting them) were commonplace in vaudeville troupes and other touring shows. By the time the fad was wearing thin nationally, it was just reaching the mountains, where rural musicians, fascinated by the mournful wail of the Hawaiian guitar, were quick to pick it up and adapt it to their own music, often combining it with the rhythmic influence of black slide-guitar style. Frankie Marvin, Cliff Carlisle, and Dorsey Dixon were all early experimenters with the instrument, which was featured on a good many of Jimmie Rodgers' records, both in blues and Hawaiian style.

By the mid-1930s the instrument—always rather quiet, its sound being directed upward, not out—was electrified and played through small amplifiers, and the combination of its wailing tone and electrically amplified hot jazz licks allowed musicians like Leon McAuliffe, with Bob Wills' Texas Playboys, to make the sound of the steel guitar (as it came to be called, because the metal bar with which it is fretted is commonly called a "steel") synonymous with the sound of country music. Even in the mid-1940s, when Gene Autry and Bob Wills were at the most "pop"-sounding stages of their respective careers, their music still contained heavy doses of the steel guitar. The name of the first musician to add foot pedals to the instrument (which bend notes upward or downward when pressed) is obscured by history, although the popular noncountry steel player Alvino Rey was using them as early as the mid-1930s. But it was not until 1954, when a Webb Pierce hit called "Slowly" contained a short, plaintive steel-guitar solo by Bud Isaacs, that the sound of those stretched and bent notes, gliding eerily upward and downward within a chord, caught the ears of musicians and fans all across rural America. Within just a year or two the pedal steel had completely surpassed its suddenly outmoded forefather, and it has since developed into the massive, complicated, two-necked, eight-pedal, four-knee lever mechanical marvel it is today. All because of a flirtation with the Hawaiian guitar over fifty years ago.

Spanish and Hawaiian influences are not the only nationalistic strains that have made their mark on what we now consider country music. There is a touch of middle European that cannot be ignored, adding a trace of seasoning to the music of both Pee Wee King (a Polish Wisconsinite) and Doc Williams (of Czech descent), WWVA radio's longtime favorite. The importance of a bit of this influence is

Hal Rugg (*left*) and Weldon Myrick playing modern versions of the pedal steel guitar on the grand Ole Opry stage. The long rods lead to the foot pedals while the knee levers also bend and push notes, often in combination. (*Grease Brothers*)

reflected in the career of Adolf Hofner, leader of a fine and still active western swing band in San Antonio, Texas, who recorded several of his selections both in English and Bohemian and today performs in that fashion, varying the music presented according to the demands of his audience and the occasion. Certainly this influence is reflected in the longtime popularity of polkas among country music audiences, a sound that probably reached its peak in the middle to late 1940s.

Another influence on country music tradition, somewhat surprisingly, was that of vaudeville and Tin Pan Alley, those bastions of all that was unreal or emotionally counterfeit as compared with the honest, gut-wrenching emotions that characterized Anglo-Celtic balladry and the country music into which it developed. Yet a catchy tune is a catchy tune, and people from the farms and mountains were no less susceptible to the charms of this music than were their urban contemporaries, given an exposure to it. So although popular song was slow in coming to the rural backwaters and was not as well received there as in the cities, there was nonetheless exposure to these ephemeral tunes, and it wasn't all that uncommon for a "pure" folk musician to follow a version of an ancient ballad like "James Harris" with a rendition of "After the Ball." As an example, it is said that Merle Travis once visited the home of a black sharecropper deep in the country while repairs were being made on a broken tour bus. Seeking inspiration, as he often did, from folk sources for his music, Travis implored the poor farmer to play the guitar he saw hanging on the wall, and despite intitial reluctance, the backcountry musician finally agreed to sing a song dear to him. His choice: the 1940 pop hit "When the Swallows Come Back to Capistrano."

Carson J. Robison, a product of the Kansas prairie, was for years associated with New York's Tin Pan Alley, writing hundreds of songs, both country and popular. He was the first country songwriter in any professional sense, for he saw his role not as the carrier of a tradition but as the creator of new popular music. (*Bob Pinson*)

A true Tin Pan Alley songwriter who wrote hits for Sophie Tucker, Fred Rose (*left*) became the greatest of all country songwriters. He developed an affection for country music in the 1930s; his songs have been recorded by every influential country music singer ever since. With him is Roy Acuff; together they founded the first publishing company in the South, Acuff-Rose, now one of the largest publishers in the world. This photo was taken in 1943, shortly after the formation of Acuff-Rose. (*Country Music Foundation Library and Media Center*)

In point of fact, many tunes from the pens of Tin Pan Alley songwriters have passed into folk tradition, simply by earning the acceptance of country singers unconcerned with definitions and origins. At first these tunes were learned—and brought gradually into tradition—through live performances, but as the popularity of first the phonograph and then radio made access to them even easier, the songs spread more rapidly, and their impact was felt with greater and greater strength throughout the Southeast and the rural Great Plains.

It is frequently said today that television is a medium of entertainment that "eats up" talent; that exposure on a scale so great quickly drains the available energies of its entertainers and writers. The same was true, on a much smaller scale, of country music in the early 1930s: The Tin Pan Alley music and the vaudeville comedy country audiences felt comfortable with was growing stale. This also held true for the "old-time" traditional folk and sentimental songs and the fiddle breakdowns that had been such a vital part of country music up to that time. What country music may have gained from the infusion of Tin Pan Alley material was then felt most strongly, for when new songs and new sounds were needed, there were creative country musicians who were able to step in and, seeing that songwriting and song styling was a craft as well as an art, write material for themselves and for others. In this sense the pounding pianos of Tin Pan Alley may have had a far deeper influence on the singer of the hills and plains than simply in the songs that became a part of tradition. It may well be that the inspiration for country songwriting was fostered and nurtured by the continued influx of "new" material from the outside.

Another recurring theme in country music is that of the saga song, the song of a specific event or tale. Because this strain derives so clearly from the British broadside ballad tradition (sheets of paper with the words to songs devoted to historical events both ancient and recent), the temptation is to include the event song within the framework of old-time music. But in a sense it does not belong there: It is a tradition probably very nearly as old as song itself, but it is a tradition that is thriving yet today, especially in the works of Tom T. Hall, whose recounting of day-to-day adventures and observations is a direct link with the saga songs and broadside ballads of the past. Long before the days of recording, songs were being written about specific events in America. "The Star-Spangled Banner," written to the tune of an old Irish drinking song, is perhaps the classic example, while "Springfield Mountain," generally considered the first known native American folk song, is an example a little closer to country music. Although "The Wreck of the Old 97" comes to mind as an early example on records, that song was actually written shortly after the original train wreck in 1903. But other contemporary events made up a considerable portion of early recorded country music: "The Death of Floyd Collins," "The Morro Castle Disaster," "The Titanic," "Bonnie Parker and Clyde Barrow," and hundreds of similar subjects were commonplace in country music in the years of its recording infancy.

One of the most colorful characters in country music, a yodeling cowboy named Red River Dave McEnery (who was once chained to a piano in a twenty-four-hour marathon songwriting session), has made a career out of writing and performing saga songs. His classic 1937 recording of "Amelia Earhart's Last Flight" was rewritten in 1960 as "The Ballad of Francis Gary Powers," and one of McEnery's latest efforts (he is a healthful and vigorous sixty) is "The Ballad of Patty Hearst." All of which goes to show that this is not a slice of history to be examined as an artifact but is a living and thriving cultural and musical tradition.

The Ballad of Patty Hearst*
by Red River Dave McEnery

(Sung to the tune of "The Battle Hymn of the Republic")

In the state of California, in the year of seventy-four,
one of God's beloved daughters heard a knock upon the door.
Violent men with flaming weapons knocked her boy friend to the
    floor,
and kidnapped Patty Hearst.

* Red River Dave McEnery, "The Ballad of Patty Hearst," © copyright 1974, Red River Dave McEnery. Used by permission.

COUNTRY ROOTS

Chorus: Beat your swords now into plowshares,
beat your swords now into plowshares.
beat your swords now into plowshares,
proclaims the Word of God. (Isa. 2:4)

Brokenhearted dad and mother prayed to God upon their knees,
then the "Liberaton Army" that was known as "Symbionese,"
made demands of giant ransom ere young Patty they'd release,
blood money for the poor.

Chorus: Beat your swords now into plowshares,
beat your swords now into plowshares,
beat your swords now into plowshares,
O read the Word of God. (Jer. 8:21)

Then there came a tape recording and the voice of Patty said,
to her darling dad and mother that she surely would be dead,
if they didn't heed the warning and distribute all that bread,
a ransom for her life.

Chorus: Beat your swords now into plowshares,
beat your swords now into plowshares,
beat your swords now into plowshares,
O heed the Word of God. (Isa. 61:1)

From the shores of "Blue Hawaii," to the harbors of Cape Cod,
God has richly blessed our nation with the harvest of her sod;
let the "Symbionesian Army" Read the blessed Word of God,
all children shall be free.

Chorus: Beat your swords now into plowshares,
beat your swords now into plowshares,
beat your swords now into plowshares,
eternal Word of God. (Gal. 6:7)

Then, there came a bloody shoot-out in the city of L.A.,
God is calling final judgement on the wicked SLA.
Was she victim? Was she willing? Only God will ever know,
sing her ballad soft and low.

Chorus: Beat your swords now into plowshares,
beat your swords now into plowshares,
beat your swords now into plowshares,
O Blessed Word of God (Matt. 7:1)

In the state of California, in the year of seventy-four,
government men discovered Patty, there in Frisco, still alive.
Was she rescued? Was she captured? Shall we pity her or blame?
Search the scriptures, once again.

Chorus: Beat your swords now into plowshares,
beat your swords now into plowshares,
beat your swords now into plowshares,
Read Matthew: seven, one.

But these are just some of the small tributary roots that have added their part to the sounds and styles of country music, that great tree of many branches. It is now nearly time to examine the main roots at length, tracing the sometimes elusive shape and form of this tree and of the roots that have nourished it.

But first a word about terminology. In any specialized field to which one is accustomed, it becomes second nature to use the jargon spoken daily by those deeply involved in that field. But although the meaning of *session*, of *A&R*, of *acoustic recording* and scores of other terms may be more than familiar to some, the same terms may become almost an incomprehensible foreign language to others, so that the original purpose of these short-cut terms is undermined and they confuse rather than clarify. Country music has its own set of these terms, and a few of the most common follow, with brief explanations, for those unfamiliar with them.

Thomas A. Edison patented the phonograph in 1877, but its use for purposes of recording and replaying music was not widely explored before the turn of the century. Until early in 1925 recording was done by speaking, singing, or playing into a large horn or horns, which condensed and channeled sound waves to a flexible diaphragm (like an eardrum), and then to a steel needle that both cut grooves and etched the wall of those groves in response to the sound onto a blank disc or cylinder. The playback of early discs was the reverse of this mechanical process. The oscillating needle cut a blank wax "master," from which "stamping parts" were cast in metal and duplicate records produced. This process is called *acoustic recording*, because the vibration of the voice or instrument is the sole force that causes the grooves in the wax to be cut (hence, "to cut a record") by the needle. During 1925 a means of recording electrically was perfected, and these recordings soon proved to be far superior in tone and fidelity to the old acoustic recordings. These *electrical recordings* were the basis of the enormously complicated system used today, although tape, not wax, has now been used for over twenty years. It was at that point that the electric microphone replaced the horn.

In addition, Edison's phonograph was made to record and play cylinder recordings, which were preferred because of the lack of variation of speed, a problem that plagued disc (flat) recordings for years but that was, of course, finally overcome. The ease of storage and shipment was probably as much a factor in the success of the disc type of recording in the battle between disc and cylinder around the turn of the century. Victor (later RCA Victor, now simply RCA) made the most popular record players of the early years, called Victrolas, and many a family listened to the latest Carter Family, Jimmie Rodgers, or Vernon Dalhart release on an old "windup Victrola," so called because it used a hand crank to wind up a large spring to supply power.

The major record companies that sprang up in the early years of this century originally had field men and talent scouts to hunt out worthy new musicians and singers, and these men eventually became known as *A&R* (for Artist and Repertoire) men. It was they who chose or helped decide which entertainers would be signed by their label, and it was their duty as well to bring the best possible song material (or repertoire) to their musical charges for recording. Their role is a bit more limited now, although it is at the same time more exalted, and they are currently called producers. Engineers, on the other hand, are the men who work at the control boards in recording situations, mixing and balancing the recording as it takes place, and today, thanks to the marvels of tape, also adding and subtracting instruments, voices, and sounds long after the original recording session (called simply a *session* by musicians and executives) has taken place. Occasionally the featured singer will take his or her own band into the recording studio, but more often than not in current industry practice a group of extremely versatile and creative men and women who are loosely defined as *session musicians* will play on the recording. The singer may take his or her own road band out on tour, but the session musicians stay in town to pick up the more lucrative recording work. This, of course, is a relatively recent phenomenon. Before the idea of country recording in the centralized location of Nashville caught stride twenty-five years ago, nearly every singer used his or her own group to record (as bluegrass singers still do), and, of course, cohesive groups were far more common and more popular then than now.

But enough of jargon, of technology, of dry detail: The living story of country music, fed by its long and diverse country roots, awaits exploration.

2
OLD-TIME MUSIC
"Carry Me Back to the Mountains"

It is a romantic and dramatic image in country music. In fact, it is an assumption on which most country music scholarship is based: that ballads, songs, and fiddle tunes of pure folk origin were discovered and preserved intact in the 1920s by the recording pioneers—the Art Satherleys, the Ralph Peers, the Frank Walkers. Likewise it is assumed that pioneer broadcasters of radio barn dances like John Lair and George D. Hay took native, authentic folk talent right off the farms and out of the hills and presented them on these broadcasts, unspoiled and unconcerned with changing musical tastes. It's as if some great folklorist/collector had gone out of his way to record and present the purest and finest of untouched mountain and prairie talent, simply for the sake of scholarship.

No doubt there were instances of preservation of totally authentic performances; but they were far from being the only or even the majority of the recordings of what was then called hillbilly music. In fact, if there was a purpose and a reason for collecting and preserving this folk art for posterity, it was to cash in on a market for nostalgia not unlike today's—hence the very name record companies frequently chose for the music itself: Old-time-music.

During the fast-paced roaring twenties, as the phonograph became more and more popular, sentimental yearning for an earlier age created a demand for recordings of gay nineties tunes. Like the city dwellers who doted on "Moonlight Bay," "Sweet Adeline," and other songs of their youth, a sizable number of farmers across the nation looked back fondly on the pleasant days of barn dances and apple peelings, long before the clatter of automobiles, the drone of airplanes, and the specter of world war had changed their lives permanently. As rural people began to acquire Victrolas and radios, it wasn't long before canny record industry executives and radio men sensed a growing market for "old-time" tunes of a rustic nature. Subsequently they sent their field representatives into the mountains to scour out musicians who could still play and sing like their fathers did in barn dance days.

PRESENTING THE SHOW
Sambo Suing Liza for a Divorce
J. E. MAINER
—— and the ——
Crazy Mountaineers
ON THIS STAGE IN PERSON

GOOD OLD TIME
SINGING, FIDDLING & BANJO PLAYING
You Have Their Records In Your Home—Now See Them
In Person—2 Hours of Fun For Everyone!

SATURDAY, MARCH 24th
At MILLING PORT SCHOOL
Sponsored by the Fire Department

Doors Open at 6:30 — — Show Starts at 7:30
Adults 75c — ADMISSION — Children 35

Of course, musicians aspiring to professionalism being what they are, there was often an attempt on the part of would-be recording artists to perform their own rendition of a hit of the day during auditions, rather than to rehash an old tune. Gene Autry is said to have auditioned with Al Jolson's "Sonny Boy" when he first came to New York in 1929. But such efforts were nearly always rejected: It was the old standard, the old fiddle tune, the sentimental ballad of the 1890s that was wanted, not the modern song. There was another sound financial reason for preferring old material: In addition to the gain expected from their nostalgia appeal, old songs could be copyrighted by the field man in a publishing company owned or controlled by him; or the songs could be written off as public domain and no royalty would be paid by the record company to either writer or publisher.

Similarly the barn dance concept was the result of an awareness on the part of sharp radio men of a large, untapped listening audience. Both John Lair, who founded the Renfro Valley Barn Dance, and George D. Hay, founder of the two most popular radio barn dances of all time, the WLS National Barn Dance in Chicago and the WSM Grand Ole Opry in Nashville, deliberately chose the rustic

Bradley Kincaid, for some reason, has to a degree been overlooked when country music pioneers are lauded, yet he was as influential as any in popularizing true country music, especially in the Northeast. The young Kentuckian made his way to Chicago in 1924, very nearly penniless, to attend college—by the time he graduated, he says with a smile, "I had a new Packard and $8,000 in the bank," not so much through personal appearances or record sales as through the phenomenal sales of his series of songbooks. After retirement from performing he opened a radio station, then a music store in Springfield, Ohio, where he still lives, golfing daily, as healthy and vigorous an eighty-year-old man as you'll find anywhere. (*Country Music Foundation Library and Media Center*)

One of the great folk singers in the solo singing tradition was Doc (his real first name is Doctor) Hopkins, whom history and fate have unfortunately chosen to overlook when plaudits for pioneers are handed out. Hopkins was a popular and influential performer on the National Barn Dance, and still lives in Chicago.

barn dance image and did everything in their power to make the musical presentations as nostalgically flavored as possible. Hay was famous, in the rapidly changing years of the 1940s, for taking Opry members aside if he felt they were getting away from this rural nostalgic image. He would remove his glasses, pinch the bridge of his nose, and repeat those famous words of his: "That's nice, but keep it down to earth."

The reason for keeping it down to earth was simple: The majority of the listeners to the Grand Ole Opry and other barn dances was a vast audience of middle-aged and elderly farming people who not only bought the products advertised on the show (Royal Crown Cola, Wall-Rite, Martha White Flour) but, especially in the case of the Opry, responded warmly to the stranger who came to their doors saying, "Hello, I'm from the National Life and Accident Insurance Company, the outfit that runs the Grand Ole Opry. . . ."

"Arkie the Arkansas Woodchopper" was practically an institution at the National Barn Dance. Guitarist, square-dance caller, folksinger, straight man, and charming personality, "Arkie" (his real name is Luther Ossenbrink) was a sparkplug on the show for years. He is retired today in rural Missouri.

Vernon Dalhart in his prime. Had his recording identity not been buried under over a hundred pseudonyms, he might well be better remembered as a founding father of country music. (*Country Music Foundation Library and Media Center*)

An advertisement for Vernon Dalhart, who, late in his life, was forced to give singing lessons for money. That he was still proud of his career on the New York stage, despite his great success in country music, is clearly shown by the choice of comments and credits in this ad, which dates from the late 1940s. Nowhere is "The Prisoner's Song" even mentioned. (*Country Music Foundation Library and Media Center*)

VERNON DALHART

VOICE PLACING

PROFESSIONAL COACHING

Bridgeport, Conn.

FOR APPOINTMENT, PHONE 4-3694

Leading Tenor

IN FOLLOWING

Operas	Oratorios	Light Operas
Il Trovatore	Holy City	Pinafore
Cavalleria	Messiah	Gondoliers
Faust	Elijah	Spring Maid
Pagliacci	Persian Garden	Fencing Master
Butterfly	Stabat Mater	Mikado
Aida	Rose Maiden	Naughty Marietta
Bohemian Girl		Paul Jones
Girl of the Golden West		Merry Widow

WHAT THE PAPERS SAY

Sang with purity and clarity and his voice floated easily over the Hippodrome. — *Alan Dale, N.Y. American.*

To sing as he sang commanded admiration, not only for his voice but for his adaptability, etc. — *Chas. Darnton, N.Y. World.*

The youthful vigor of his voice makes him an appropriate choice for the part; and besides he plays it so well. — *N.Y. Times.*

This good tenor was exceptionally pleasing. — *N.Y. Journal.*

He has a charming voice and knows how to use it. — *N.Y. Sun.*

Sang the tenor hero's role with ease. — *N.Y. Herald.*

An exceptionally good tenor. — *N.Y. Press.* Sang beautifully. — *N.Y. Tribune.*

His tones were bright, musical, and finely charming. — *Newark News.*

Sang his way into the affection of the audience. — *Montreal Herald.*

An excellent tenor voice and knows how to use it. — *New Orleans Item.*

One of the most accomplished artists the Buffalonian ever had. — *Buffalo Courier.*

Sang in a most convincing manner. — *Boston Post.*

A tenor voice of great purity. — *Indianapolis Star.*

A splendid tenor voice. — *Washington Herald.*

A remarkably fine tenor. — *Boston American.*

An excellent tenor voice. — *Richmond Times.*

A sweet, clear tenor voice. — *Sacramento Bee.*

A fine lyric tenor. — *Seattle Daily Times.*

Vocally delightful. — *Baltimore Star.*

An excellent tenor. — *Toronto Globe.*

George D. Hay in the early to middle 1920s, at the start of his successful career in broadcasting, which was to include the formation and naming of both the National Barn Dance and the Grand Ole Opry. (*Country Music Foundation Library and Media Center*)

George D. Hay (ca. 1925), who called himself "The Solemn Old Judge," started the National Barn Dance in 1924 and the Grand Ole Opry in 1925. A stern traditionalist, his constant admonitions to experimenting musicians in the 1940s, the decade of flux, were "Keep it close to the ground" and "Keep it down to earth, boys."

The makeup of casts of early radio barn dances is a fascinating study, especially in its regional variation. The Opry, for instance, stuck strictly with string bands from its beginnings in 1925 through the next ten years, which synchronizes rather accurately with the period (ca. 1935) when country music began to break away from the image of nostalgia that had fostered its initial popularity and began to be a commercial musical form, with more emphasis on new songs and new styles within the older tradition. Some stylistic differences existed among shows: While the Opry, with its largely southeastern listening audience, was for the most part composed of

680 KC
Affiliated with NBC

5000 WATTS
Member NAB

WPTF RADIO CO., Raleigh, N. C.

| Vol. 1 | Wednesday, June 24, 1936 | No. 16 |

THE COUNTRY DOCTOR

Some inside glimpses of the lives of the celebrated Dionne quintuplets will be given to radio listeners of WPTF by Dr. Allan Roy Dafoe, internationally famous as their personal physician, when he gives a series of talks as guest speaker on the Carnation Contented Program, beginning Monday, June 29, at 9:00 p.m., E.S.T., over the NBC network. The modest country doctor will speak on the program once each month during June, July, August, and September, while the regular musical portion of the program, featuring Morgan Eastman's orchestra, the Carnation Quartet, and the Lullaby Lady, will continue to add joy to the famous program, sponsored by Carnation Milk.

ONE MAN'S FAMILY

With eighteen "books" of thirteen episodes each, or more than 1,750,000 words, already written and broadcast on the One Man's Family programs, presented by Tenderleaf Tea, Carlton Morse, the author, launches another "book" on Wednesday, July 1, from 7:00 to 7:30 p.m., E.S.T., over WPTF and the NBC-Red network, with a general picture of how things are progressing in the scattered family of Henry Barbour. Tenderleaf Tea is to be congratulated on its popular program, a dramatic, human picture of a typical American family of this generation.

TOWN HALL TONIGHT

Colonel Stoopnagle and Budd will take over the Town Hall Tonight broadcast on Wednesday, July 1, from 8:00 to 9:00 p.m., E.S.T., over the NBC-WPTF network, when Fred Allen leaves for fourteen weeks vacation. The Colonel hasn't the faintest idea what he and Budd will do with Fred's full-hour show but the usual amateur group will appear, as will the Town Hall Quartet and Peter Van Steeden's orchestra, and the manufacturers of Sal Hepatica and Ipana are certain to win more loyal fans to their famous "Smile Brigade."

AIN'T WE CRAZY?

THE CRAZY MOUNTAINEERS

If it's hillbilly harmony at its happiest that you like, the Crazy Mountaineers are on the air to serve you. They're sponsored daily except Sunday at WPTF by Crazy Water Crystals, manufactured by the Crazy Water Hotel Company, of Mineral Wells, Texas, and not a day passes when the studio is not jammed with fans who have driven in to town to see and hear their favorites on the air. Crazy Water Crystals, a natural mineral water product, has won a secure place on the family medicine chest, both through its health-giving action and the happiness and laughter bestowed freely by its Mountaineer representatives. The boys are widely known for their Bluebird recordings and have made quite a name for themselves through their original compositions. Each night, the Crazy Mountaineers appear in person in neighboring communities with their own show titled "Crazy Capers," while every Saturday night the hour from 9:30 to 10:30 has been set aside as Crazy Barn Dance time, with the Mountaineers and a whole gang of associate hillbillie cutting up in a nearby village schoolhouse, much to the joy of their show audience and radio fans everywhere.

JULY FOURTH FIREWORKS

North Carolina's second primary on July 4th will see the culmination of one of the State's most intensive election campaigns, and once again WPTF's airlanes will be dedicated throughout the night to a broadcast of balloting returns, for the benefit of voters who wish to listen in. The station will remain on the air for an indefinite period on the night of the Fourth, with a private ticker of an internationally known news agency installed in the studio, rendering prompt, accurate service on returns gathered from every county in North Carolina. WPTF invites all within its listening radius to tune in and follow the voting trend.

MUSIC BY GROFE

Through the courtesy of the Ford dealers of America, WPTF is privileged to present every Tuesday and Thursday evening at 7:45 "The Ford V-8 Revue," featuring the distinctive music of the celebrated composer-conductor, Ferde Grofe and his orchestra. Supplementing its network feature, the Fred Waring Broadcast, heard over WPTF every Friday evening at 8:00 o'clock, the local Ford programs are winning more and more friends not only to entertainment that is truly different, but to a knowledge of motoring that is economical.

KELVINATOR DEALER HAPPY

Because it gets results, WPTF's Musical Clock is adding more friends and keeping old friends every day. The Lewis Sporting Goods Company of Raleigh, dealers for Kelvinator Electric Refrigerators, Universal Ranges, and Easy Washers and Ironers, have demonstrated their full approval of their quarter-hour block on the Clock Hour by signing a new contract for an indefinite period, and with WPTF's fan mail growing in volume each week, offering listener proof that the program is reaching attentive ears, the sponsor is due for even more success.

square-dance bands who occasionally sang a "shout tune" (a fast, rousing, sing-along footstomper) or a hymn but in general simply played the old fiddle tunes learned from their grandfathers, the National Barn Dance on WLS in Chicago (which predated the Opry by a year) had a much more varied content, in an attempt at reaching a broader cross-section of its primarily midwestern and Great Plains audience. For every old-time act like Lulu Belle and Scotty or Arkie the Arkansas Woodchopper, there was a Henry Burr, a big-voiced singer of sentimental and semiclassical tunes who had been recording since the days of Edison cylinders; or there was a pianist like Grace Wilson; or a novelty band like the Hoosier Hot Shots. Regardless of the techniques and artists used to attract as large a share of the audience as possible, the formula was still the same: sentimental, nostalgic, "old-time" music, guaranteed to remind the agrarian listener of a happier, simpler, more carefree time.

Much the same attitude prevailed in the recording end of the music business. The Carter Family and Jimmie Rodgers, who first recorded for Victor Records within days of each other in 1927, both emphasized the traditional musical virtues of their respective regions: Rodgers the sentimental ballads and black-influenced blues of central Mississippi; the Carter Family the strait-laced, stiff-backed, religious-oriented music of the deepest Appalachian hollows. Also recorded at that time was a blind singer with a big, rough-hewn voice so charged with emotion it sounded like he was shouting to God from a mountaintop. His name was Alfred Karnes, and he later disappeared back into the hills never to be heard from again.

Most histories list Uncle Jimmy Thompson as the first performer on the Grand Ole Opry, but a small minority insist, with some justification, that it was Dr. Humphrey Bate and his Possum Hunters, a fine old-time string band. That's Dr. Bate (a real M.D., who, like all the early Opry cast, simply played the barn dance on the weekend) holding the dog. (*Country Music Foundation Library and Media Center*)

The original Gully Jumpers. *Left to right*: Roy Hardison, Charlie Arrington, Bert Hutcherson, Paul Warmack, and Fred Shriver.

The Crook Brothers Band, 1932. The Crook "brothers" (they are actually cousins), Herman and Lewis, are on the top row, and continue to play the Opry every Saturday night. Seated are (*left to right*) Blythe Poteet, Kirk McGee, and Bill Etters. (*Country Music Foundation Library and Media Center*)

Ernest V. "Pop" Stoneman was a recording pioneer who remained active in country music until his death in 1968. He recorded for an amazing number of labels in the 1920s and 1930s, and then again with his children, known professionally as the Stoneman Family, in the 1960s. He is shown here with an early (1928) group in Boaz, Alabama. *Left to right*: Ives Edwards, George Stoneman, Eck Dunford, Ernest V. Stoneman, Balen Frost, and Ms. Frost's brother.

Tent shows became extremely popular in the 1930s and 1940s, none more popular than the Opry's—here's what one looked like to the fan of the time. (*Country Music Foundation and Media Center*)

The stars of the National Barn Dance pose together in a scene from the 1944 film *The National Barn Dance. Left to right* are Lulu Belle and Scotty, the Hoosier Hot Shots, Pat Buttram, and "Arkie the Arkansas Woodchopper." (*National Screen Service Corp.*)

The date of these famous recording sessions, conducted by Ralph Peer, on August 2–4, 1927, is a monumental one in the history of country music, but there were recordings of country music bands and songs, and even a million-selling record, predating Peer's landmark sessions. It is generally thought that Eck Robertson was the first country musician to have been recorded, fiddling "Sally Goodin'" and "Arkansas Traveler" for Victor in 1922.

Then in 1925 a moderately successful light-opera singer—who since as early as 1916 had occasionally been recording sentimental tunes like "Can't Yo' Heah Me Callin' Caroline?"—tried his hand at a country song, and his two-sided hit, "The Prisoner's Song"/"The Wreck of the Old 97," became, in all probability, the first million-selling record of all time. He was Vernon Dalhart, and it may well be that he sold more records than any other country singer, for he recorded for a wide variety of labels utilizing well over one hundred pseudonyms. In fact, the name Vernon Dalhart is itself yet another pseudonym for Marion Try Slaughter, a Texan who chose the names of two nearby towns in the Lone Star State, Vernon and Dalhart,

Country music pioneers in every sense, the Carter Family are among the handful of influential people who have shaped the direction in which country music has evolved. Their singing, their playing, their collecting of songs—all these helped make country music what it is today. (*Country Music Foundation Library and Media Center*)

for his stage name. Although he was the first hillbilly "star" in a national sense, Dalhart's true home territory was the New York stage, and this fact, combined with the overpowering number of names he recorded under and labels on which he appeared, has led to neglect of the memory of this man. His recordings with fiddle, harmonica, and guitar sound a bit stiff but are just as "country" as anything else of the period; his sound, for all his activity in light opera and the New York stage, was on record distinctively and decidedly country, a fact often overlooked today.

Nevertheless, the early groups who were recorded (except for Rodgers and Dalhart, the emphasis was heavily on groups) were authentic mountain or farm people whose isolation helped them preserve older musical forms desired by nostalgia-minded record companies. Yet many of these groups were far more sophisticated than their records would have them appear to us today. Clayton McMichen and his Georgia Wildcats, for example, added a clarinet to the band as early as the middle to late 1920s, and Kansan Carson J. Robison, famous as a songwriter as well as a performer, wrote the pop hit "Barnacle Bill the Sailor" as well as early country classics like "Little Green Valley" and "Left My Gal in the Mountains." In fact, relatively few of these early bands were as isolated from outside culture as we may be led to believe: Their recordings reflect both their own desire to stay within a tradition and the desire of their record companies to maintain their appeal for a largely middle-aged, rural, nostalgia-buying public.

But there are just so many old songs, so many versions of old songs, to be recorded and played over the air. By 1932 the combination of the economic woes of the Great Depression and the coinciding boom period of radio cut record sales to 10 percent of what they had been in the late twenties. Something—anything—was needed and sought out by record company men to stave off the bankruptcy that had killed so many of the fine old labels, including Paramount, Gennett, and the original Columbia. It was at this point that the obvious suggested itself to many: Use new material in traditional style. (This concept has today given us country music's continued emphasis on the songwriter and perhaps the whole star system itself.)

Caroline and Mary, the DeZurik Sisters, were a popular yodeling team of the 1930s and 1940s. They added the athletic tendencies of the Swiss yodel to the blue yodel of Jimmie Rodgers, setting the style for a host of yodeling cowboys and cowgirls to come. Interestingly, when they came to the Opry from the National Barn Dance, they changed their distinctively European name for a much more rural one: The Cackle Sisters. (*Country Music Foundation Library and Media Center*)

The Opry cast in the early 1930s. Some notable bands and individuals include the Delmore Brothers, Lewis Crook, and Deford Bailey in the back row; Herman Crook, Sam and Kirk McGee with Arthur Smith, and George D. Hay in the third row; Dr. Humphrey Bate's Possum Hunters, Uncle Dave Macon, and the Gully Jumpers in the second row. (*Country Music Foundation Library and Media Center*)

The Fruit Jar Drinkers, living out their band name as they take a nip from a fruit jar in the late 1920s. (*Country Music Foundation Library and Media Center*)

Frankie More's Log Cabin Boys (ca. 1930s) were popular in the Louisville area for years, and the band generated several musicians who were to become important later: Standing on the *right* and kneeling on the *left* are the Callahan Brothers, and kneeling at the *right* is Pee Wee King.

Of course, the movement toward newer song material did not occur just overnight: Carson Robison had been writing songs with success since the middle 1920s, as had another New York-based writer, Bob Miller. Jimmie Rodgers relied heavily on "new" material, much of it from the pen of his sister-in-law, Elsie McWilliams; and even "The Prisoner's Song" was a recent composition in its time. But as the 1930s moved on, clearly country music style was shifting away from loose fiddle bands toward solo performers who wrote—or were at least able to come up with—material of their own, like Gene Autry and Jimmie Davis.

It was during this era that country music began developing its many commercial branches, reaching out for different segments of a constant audience and for new audiences as well: Singing cowboys began to come to the fore in imitation of Gene Autry, and southwestern dance bands like Bob Wills and his Texas Playboys attracted new audiences in dance halls and on record. Yet the Southeast, for whatever reason, tended to remain musically conservative, more traditional, and the changes that came over the business and the music in general came more slowly in that region. The Grand Ole Opry, for instance, hired only two singing groups in the early 1930s, the Vagabonds and the Delmore Brothers, before finally relenting to Pee Wee King's big cowboy band, the Golden West Cowboys, in 1937. Later the Opry signed the singer/leaders of tradition-oriented but musically energetic, inventive, and refreshing string bands: Roy Acuff in 1938 and Bill Monroe in 1939.

For the Southeast, the popular music of the 1930s was a stylistic blend of the old Carter Family (who were still quite popular) mixed with the feeling of the string band and, not surprisingly, with the sound of family and brother groups, who grew up with strange new instruments, the guitar and mandolin, and learned to match these instruments and their voices to the songs and hymns they had absorbed in their youth. It is this rough collection of groups, sounds, and styles that remained so (relatively) traditional that its contents are still identified together as old time.

The Pickard Family, an early Opry group. *Left to right*: Mother, Ruth, Little Ann, Dad, Charlie, and Bub. The photo is signed "Peruna," which was a patent medicine guaranteed to cure all ills, and longtime sponsor of the Pickards. (*Bob Pinson*)

Asher Sizemore and Little Jimmie were a very popular act in early radio and spent several years on the Grand Ole Opry in the 1930s. The cover of their 1936 song folio shows the deliberate attempt to capture the warmth and flavor of an earlier, more nostalgic era.

An early cast of the National Barn Dance, posed near Renfro Valley, Kentucky, where many of the cast were from. You can tell the picture is a composite: Red Foley appears to be wooing Lulu Belle at the far *left*, and is also playing bass with the Cumberland Ridge Runners at *right*. Likewise, Karl Davis is fiddling to Harty Taylor's accompaniment on the *left*, while the same two make up the guitar and mandolin section of the Cumberland Ridge Runners on the *right*. Leaning jauntily against the fence with his hand in his belt is John Lair, pioneer broadcaster who went on from the National Barn Dance to form the Renfro Valley Barn Dance.

The longtime stars of the National Barn Dance, Lulu Belle and Scotty, most famous for their "Have I Told You Lately That I Love You?" Today they live in Spruce Pine, North Carolina, where Lulu Belle is now a representative in the North Carolina legislature. (*Country Music Foundation Library and Media Center*)

In the early days of radio, it was not at all uncommon for band members to switch and shift from one band to another. This band was called the Home Town Boys, but Bill Helms (*left*) led his own popular group he called the Upson County Band, while Riley Puckett (on guitar) and Gid Tanner (on fiddle at *right*) were the two most famous members of the Skillet Lickers, an extremely important and influential early string band. This shot dates from around 1931. (*Bob Pinson*)

Clayton McMichen, who in his later years preferred to be called Pappy, added a trumpet to his band in the mid-1920s, buddied around with Jimmie Rodgers (he wrote or co-wrote several Rodgers' songs, including "Peach Picking Time in Georgia," and led a fine old-time string band called the Georgia Wildcats for many years.

The Cumberland Ridge Runners, extremely popular both as a group and as individuals on the early National Barn Dance. *Left to right*: Slim Miller, John Lair, Karl Davis, Linda Parker ("The Sunbonnet Girl"), Red Foley, and Harty Taylor. John Lair went on to form the Renfro Valley Barn Dance, while Karl and Harty were one of the finest and most neglected duets of the 1930s: Their compositions include "I'm Just Here to Get My Baby Out of Jail" and "The Prisoner's Dream." Linda Parker died suddenly in her prime, and Red Foley, of course, went on to become one of country music's greatest stars. (*Country Music Foundation Library and Media Center*)

Fiddlin' Arthur Smith and Jimmy Wakely. Smith's long and varied career included stints with Sam and Kirk McGee on the Opry, as Arthur Smith and the Dixieliners, and shots in several Jimmy Wakely movies as the leading cowboy fiddler. Smith was tremendously influential on the whole generation of fiddlers who followed him, and his bluesy style was widely copied.

Within this early period no new name such as western swing or honky-tonk was ever developed, and indeed this type of country music has remained so firmly attached to the basics from which it originally came that it wears its old-fashioned label with considerable pride even to this day.

Two of the most popular groups of the era were brother acts with the last names Mainer and Monroe. The Mainers, a fiddler named J.E. and a banjo player named Wade, were to lead their own groups by the end of the decade, but while together their 1936 recording of "Maple on the Hill" was a huge success, as was "What Would You Give in Exchange for Your Soul?" by two brothers from Rosine, Kentucky, Bill and Charlie Monroe. Although their recording career as a duet lasted only two short years, they made a tremendous impact on the history of country music through their fiery musicianship, and Bill eventually went on to develop one of the most popular of country music's subgenres, bluegrass.

To simply list the brother and family groups from the 1930s on would be an enormous undertaking, but a few are especially important. For example, the Blue Sky Boys (Bill and Earl Bolick), who began recording for Bluebird Records (Victor's low-priced label) at the ages of sixteen and eighteen, became especially loved during the folksong revival of the 1950s and 1960s because of their haunting interpretation of early British and American ballads such as "Mary of the Wild Moor" and "The

As brother teams sometimes do, the Mainers split up, and banjo-playing Wade went on to form another extremely popular string band called the Sons of the Mountaineers. In this 1940 shot, showing the stacks of mail received at WPTF in Raleigh, the band consists of Bill Hall (*top left*) and Clyde Moody on guitars (Moody was later to become one of the big stars of the 1940s—his "Shenandoah Waltz" sold some three million records for King); Wade on banjo; and Steve Ledford on fiddle. Wade Mainer, a dignified, gentle, and gracious man, now lives in Flint, Michigan, where he has worked for some thirty years since retirement from the music business. Clyde Moody is still active in the music business, often playing bluegrass festivals (he joined Bill Monroe not long after this shot was taken and was on the Blue Grass Boys' first recordings in 1941).

Butcher's Boy," although their full repertoire extended to hymns, sentimental ballads of the 1890s, and a few of their own compositions. Their mournful, moving harmony set singing standards for years to come and was inspirational to many later groups.

The Delmore Brothers are often remembered for introducing the boogie and the blues into the country duet, but actually they were thoroughly self-trained musicians who were largely responsible for the more careful, controlled approach to duet singing that followed them. They sang soft and sweet, with precise harmony, and both died much too young.

It's all a matter of opinion, of course, but perhaps the greatest of all country duets was a relatively late one, the Louvin Brothers. Though they achieved their greatest popularity in the 1950s, Charlie, the younger of the two, went on to forge a still-successful solo career after the death of his brother, Ira, in 1965. Influenced heavily by the Blue Sky Boys and the Delmore Brothers, the Louvins were a smooth yet spine-chilling duet, combining intricate harmonies with the most haunting qualities of intense mountain expression. There is no greater example of the repressed intensity of country music than the Louvins' recording of "When I Stop Dreaming"—that is the soul of country music, the raw, intense, exposed nerve endings that express so eloquently the pain inherent and unavoidable in the human condition.

Wilma Lee and Stoney Cooper, one of country music's most popular husband–wife duets. Their early records are masterpieces of old-time mountain music, and although they developed a more commercial sound in the mid-1950s, they never lost their straightforward, honest mountain quality and have gotten something of a second wind lately with appearances at bluegrass festivals. Wilma Lee is one of country music's greatest traditional female singers. (*Wilma Lee and Stoney Cooper*)

The Delmore Brothers, Rabon (*left*) and Alton, in the early 1930s. The first of the brother duets to carefully study music and harmony, their thoughtful, gentle music is a delight. Rabon died rather suddenly at the age of thirty-six in 1952, while the team was still very popular, and Alton retired to his native Alabama, where he died in 1964, leaving a recently discovered unfinished autobiography called *Truth Is Stranger Than Publicity*. (*Lionel Delmore*)

Johnny and Jack and the Tennessee Mountain Boys. Longtime fixtures of the music business, they finally put together a string of hits in the early 1950s, like "Ashes of Love," "I Can't Tell My Heart That," and "Poison Love." After Jack Anglin's death in an auto accident in 1963, Johnny Wright combined his show with that of his wife, Kitty Wells. Up on the cowcatcher are two famous sidemen, Paul Warren (*left*) and Shot Jackson. After fifteen years with Johnny and Jack, Warren has worked the past twenty with Flatt and Scruggs, remaining with Lester Flatt after the breakup of the team. Jackson, a famous dobro player in his own right, cofounded the world-famous Sho-Bud Guitars in Nashville. (*Bob Pinson*)

Mac and Bob (Lester McFarland [*left*] and Bob Gardner) met at the Kentucky School for the Blind and, of the earliest duets, forged a career that was to last over a quarter-century. They began on WNOX in Knoxville but achieved their greatest popularity on WLS in Chicago. Their singing tended to be as stiff and formal as this 1931 photo, but they were tremendously influential on later "brother" mandolin–guitar duets, both in style and especially in repertoire.

But brother acts were just a small part of the total spectrum that traditional or "old-time" country music spanned in the years before the war. Family groups were popular in schools and churches long before the Carter Family stepped up to a Victor microphone that historic August day in 1927. In fact, the Opry had a long-popular group called the Pickard Family on the air at about the same time the Carters first recorded. Moreover, the Leary Family, from Valley Head, West Virginia, was one of the most popular groups of their region and their era, and they produced a daughter with a big, emotional voice named Wilma Lee. When she married a handsome young fiddler named Stoney Cooper, she stepped from one country music traditon to another, that of the husband–wife duet, a style which they, as Wilma Lee and Stoney Cooper, are continuing to carry on at the Grand Ole Opry to this day. Lulu Belle and Scotty were another such team, their smoother sound having gained them a large following in the Midwest over the WLS National Barn Dance. And the great and legendary singer Molly O'Day started performing with her husband, Lynn Davis, as did one of the greats of country-gospel music of the 1950s, Martha Carson. In general, the wife was the featured singer, with the husband providing both instrumental support and vocal harmony. The list of

Resplendent Dolly Parton came from a dirt-poor East Tennessee family to become one of country music's biggest stars. Popular success has not diminished her sensitivity and feeling for old-time country music, and there is a refreshing touch of the traditional in her contemporary and popular music and songwriting. (*Grease Brothers*)

Dolly Parton and Porter Wagoner. (*Grease Brothers*)

names, some of them alliterative goes on: Bonnie Lou and Buster, Joe and Rose Lee Maphis, Smokey and Dottie Swan, Annie Lou and Danny, and hundreds of others. But Wilma Lee and Stoney Cooper and Joe and Rose Maphis are just about the only big-time remnants of this once-flourishing type of musical entertainment, although Porter Wagoner's duets with Dolly Parton tend to partially preserve the sound of the tradition. Certainly the male–female duet is still a popular means of musical expression, but nowadays it is mostly performed by two "stars" in their own right (like Conway Twitty and Loretta Lynn, George Jones and Tammy Wynette) rather than by a cohesive family unit.

Women singers in general have had an important role in traditional country music, dating from Sara and Maybelle Carter through Dolly Parton, who retains much of traditional country style in her currently popular sound—one of the gifted and sensitive few who are able to combine the old and the new. But women singers and musicians in early country music were rare, for if the career of musician was considered unsavory for men, it was considered unthinkable for women. Traveling in a family band was acceptable, but it took a good many years before women were accepted as solo singers with their own bands. In fact, Kitty Wells, often referred to by the media as the Queen of Country Music, sang off and on as a guest in her husband's popular band, Johnny and Jack, for about ten years before she stepped out into the limelight on her own in the early 1950s.

Roy Acuff frequently tells a story that illustrates the prevailing feeling toward women in early country music bands in relating how his longtime sidekick, band member, comedian, and tenor singer Bashful Brother Oswald got his stage name. It seems that in the early 1940s Roy hired a banjo-playing comedian named Rachel Veach, who was carefully called Cousin Rachel, but even so Acuff began to get fan mail that was extremely negative toward his carrying a young woman on his show. The pressure mounted to the point where Acuff considered dropping Rachel from the act, but he hit upon a solution: He paired Rachel with his comedian and dobro player Pete Kirby, calling them "Cousin Rachel and her great big bashful brother Oswald," a name that stayed with Kirby long after Rachel Veach left the Smoky Mountain Boys. From that point on there was no longer any adverse reaction to Rachel's presence from Acuff's loyal fans. As long as it appeared she was in the protective company of her big brother, all was well.

Although women singers had, on occasion, been popular before the war—Louise Massey is an example, as is Patsy Montana, the first woman to have a million-selling record ("I Want to Be a Cowboy's Sweetheart")—it wasn't until the success of Kitty Wells that the field opened up for them. Wells (who took her stage name from an old folk song; her real name is Muriel Deason) sang in a soft, sorrowful style, as opposed to the exhortative styles of Molly O'Day and Wilma Lee Cooper, and although her voice itself betrayed little emotion, her plaintive tone was and is extremely moving and affective. Beyond this she was the first important woman singer to tackle in song the issues that so disturbed postwar America: infidelity, divorce, and drinking. Her "It Wasn't God That Made Honky-Tonk Angels" was but one of dozens of songs that reflected the trauma of America's postwar return to normalcy,

Roy Acuff, "The King of Country Music," around 1941 with the Smoky Mountain Boys. *Left to right:* Velma Williams, Jesse Easterday, Pete Kirby, Jimmy Riddle, Rachel Veach, Acuff and Lonnie Wilson.

and her willingness to deal frankly with these new and emotion-charged problems, combined with her touching singing style, earned her the title of Queen of Country Music—a title that she should never have to relinquish despite a lack of hit records over the last decade. Kitty Wells not only opened up a new subject matter for the tradition-oriented Southeast but she paved the way for the acceptance of women singers in general, something that was long overdue in country music. Moreover, she directly influenced the styles of many important women singers who followed her, Loretta Lynn the most prominent.

The string-band tradition, like most country music traditions, was not quick to die out. In fact, it is still alive and kicking rather strongly, if not commercially. The early days of the Opry in particular were ruled by string bands, a reign broken only

A beautiful and young Kitty Wells. For years a part of her husband Johnny Wright's band (Johnny's playing bass, at *left*), she finally stepped out into her own in the early 1950s, becoming the "Queen of Country Music" with her sorrowful voice and unflinching treatment of harsh, modern themes. The fiddler is a young Chet Atkins, long a staff musician at Knoxville's WNOX.

Jimmie Davis and W. Lee O'Daniel weren't the only country singers to catch political fever. Here Roy Acuff makes a telling point while stumping for Governor of Tennessee in the 1948 election. A Republican in a traditionally Democratic state, he made a strong showing in his losing effort.

Sam (*right*) and Kirk McGee shortly before Sam's death, venerable and beloved members of the Grand Ole Opry cast. (*Grease Brothers*)

by the harmonica performances of Deford Bailey and the comic routines of Uncle Dave Macon. Gradually, however, a shift took place. First came the Vagabonds, a smooth-singing trio, and then the intricate, careful harmony of the Delmore Brothers; not a fiddle among them. The Missouri Mountaineers replaced the Vagabonds, then Zeke Clements, the Alabama Cowboy, jumped on the Opry bandwagon, and while Pee Wee King's Golden West Cowboys featured a fiddler, they were hardly a fiddle band. Musical tastes and expectations were changing across the South, and Dr. Humphrey Bate's Possum Hunters, the Crook Brothers Band, and the Gully Jumpers were unable to fill such a broad spectrum of musical needs as was developing among Opry listeners. It is a tribute, however, to the astonishing loyalty of country music fans that two string bands, with many of their original members, still play regularly at the Opry (the Crook Brothers and the Gully Jumpers), as did Sam McGee up until his death in August, 1975, at the age of eighty-two. Although their role is largely confined simply to playing backup music for the highly visual square dancers, they still can be heard every Saturday night as they have been for nearly fifty years.

When Roy Acuff reached the Opry in 1938, he came basically as the fiddling leader of a string band; it was some time before he became primarily a singer and a bandleader. Tremendous public response to his rendition of "The Great Speckled Bird" led him to realize that his career contained more potential than that of a fiddler who led a string band; that singing and showmanship were able to fill needs that square dance music was not. Similarly, when Bill Monroe joined the Opry a year after Acuff, he brought with him a band that contained the elements of bluegrass rhythm and emphasized the vocal style that was to become bluegrass but that basically was a four-piece string band, featuring Monroe's mandolin playing (legendary even then) nearly as much as the fiddle. The shift here is evident: The Opry was hiring string bands in the old tradition, but string bands fronted by singers.

The next Opry acquisition in 1943 was part of a logical and historically revolutionary development: Ernest Tubb, with electric guitar and steel guitar. Thus the string-band tradition turned into the singing-star tradition in the space of a few short years. The use of the Opry to illustrate this change is simply a convenience—no slighting of great non-Opry old-time groups like the Skillet Lickers, Charlie Poole's North Carolina Ramblers, the Blue Ridge Entertainers, or any other of a hundred fine and influential groups is intended. Opry history illustrates in miniature the change occurring on a national basis, and it wasn't long before the traditional string band was a thing of the past, except for a few continuing evocative moments on the Grand Ole Opry stage.

Yet while the traditional string band was quietly fading into history, a string-band sound rooted in tradition was coming to the fore. Combining Bill Monroe's high, lonesome singing, driving rhythm, and bluesy choice of improvisatory notes with the dazzling playing of an inventive young kid from North Carolina named Earl Scruggs (who was only nineteen when he joined Monroe's Blue Grass Boys in 1945), this all-acoustic string music became a bastion for traditionalists, yet excited new listeners daily from the mid-1940s to the present. So in a sense bluegrass carries on the tradition of the string band in its reverence for tradition and deliberate unwillingness to be changed by the pressures of more commercial musical forms.

When came the so-called "folk-song revival" of the middle to late 1950s, urban northerners began to feel the charm, the directness, the utter lack of pretentiousness, the inherent sincerity and earthiness of what they started to call "old-timey" string-band music, not fully realizing that the "Old-Time Music" printed on those funny old Paramount and Gennett and Conqueror 78s was meant to evoke sentimental longing for a time yet another thirty or forty years earlier than the date the discs were recorded. Nevertheless, groups like the New Lost City Ramblers were serious about and dedicated to this music, which spoke so strongly of a time past, and they consciously and carefully transferred what they heard on scratchy 78s to live performance. Through their efforts, the New Lost City Ramblers in particular introduced thousands upon thousands of young, musically disenchanted collegians to the delights of "old-timey" southern string-band music. They presented this music seriously—rarely tongue-in-cheek as it is all too easy for the outsider to do—and it was quickly understood by most of their audience that this was music of worth and of value. It is hard to underestimate the importance of the New Lost City Ramblers in opening up the eyes and ears of so many educated, citified northerners (many of whom, in imitation of the Ramblers, have gone to form string bands of their own) to traditional country music (and, as many continued to explore the music, a number of the other branches as well). While it cannot be said of string-band music, as it can of bluegrass, that its popularity is at an all-time peak, there is still considerable interest in this music. It is even getting some national attention, through appearances on national television by groups like the Highwoods String Band. Though you may never hear their records played on your local country radio station, they are available, for a host of small companies with names like County, Rounder, Folkways, and Old Homestead have sprung up to fill the need of a relatively small but eager buying public for old-time (as well as bluegrass) records, both by urban revivalists and authentic country musicians, some of whom have been rediscovered in recent years and recorded as they sound today.

It has been said before and it will be said again: The country music fan is nothing if he is not loyal, and, seemingly, there will always be a market (although it will always, in all likelihood, be small) for old-time country music, particularly string-band music. This musical style, the basics out of which most of later country music was to develop, will never die, for there always are just enough people who want to hear not only what Charlie Poole, the Callahan Brothers, James and Martha Carson, or Pop Stoneman did in the past, but what the Hotmud Family has to say to us today. It is truly valid music, not only for its time but, in that country music often speaks across a broad spectrum of time and of the human condition, for our time as well.

3
BLUES
"Everybody's Had the Blues"

Imagine, for a moment, the feelings of a young boy of another age and place; a musician of 1890, just learning a few shaky fiddle tunes from his father, deep in the mountains of southwestern Virginia or eastern Kentucky. Slight, blue-eyed, with sallow skin so thin you can almost see through it, he has taken a long hike this morning to see the great wonder being constructed, word of which has filtered back through the dark hollows: a huge railroad trestle, spanning the gorge. He reaches the area after miles of hiking, on the lunch hour of the workers, and what he sees and hears there is a dramatic shock that will leave an indelible imprint on his memory and his psyche: men with sweaty, shiny black and brown faces, lounging around eating and talking, a few gathered near a fellow section hand who was picking, sometimes deftly, sometimes crudely, a big, rounded box with a hole in the top, strung with gut like a fiddle, but so big you had to hold it upright in your lap instead of under your chin. Its sound, though slightly out of tune, is deeper and richer than the young mountaineer had ever imagined an instrument could be, filling and supporting, ducking under and sparkling over the voice of the singer—a pain-haunted, rich, slurred voice also wildly unfamiliar. But the sense and the mood and the feel of the music he hears that day is provocative and evocative, and at once a bond is formed between the mountain white and the black musician, a bond of sympathy and understanding of hard times held in common. It was this encounter that brought the guitar and the blues to the mountains and to country music.

A quick glance at today's music business—its activity, focus, and its all-important measure of success, the "charts"—is all that is necessary to see immediately how far apart are the worlds of country and soul. In a nation so rapidly undergoing—in one of the media's pet words—polarization, no other single indicator, not even dress or speech patterns, tends to crystalize these polarized groups and attitudes into increasingly rigid positions as much as music.

Sam McGee, who learned his celebrated finger-style guitar not long after the turn of the century, was featured regularly on the Grand Ole Opry until his death in a farm accident at the age of eighty-two in August 1975. (*Grease Brothers*)

Yet this was not always so, and while there is occasional musical cross-pollenization today, as recently as fifty years ago there was frequently not all that much difference in the music of rural blacks and whites. In the cities, yes, the differences were already great and growing greater, but in rural America musical exchanges were frequent and even commonplace among both black and white musicians.

In fact, it wasn't until around the turn of the century that the guitar—the sine qua non of country music—was introduced to the hills, and while most instruments were bought through the omnipresent Sears Roebuck or Montgomery Ward catalogs by mail, the use and application of the instrument was taught, to a large degree, by black section workers and railroaders who brought their guitars with them while laying railroad tracks in the mountains. Sam and Kirk McGee, for example, learned their celebrated guitar style from the black section workers who took breaks at the little general store, just outside of Nashville, owned by their father. In fact, the McGees claim there is little difference between the way they play today and the playing of two black railroaders they learned from over sixty years ago. It was two brothers named Stewart who taught the two eager McGee youngsters finger-style blues guitar, a style Sam McGee pioneered in white recorded rural music.

And the McGees were far from being the only ones so influenced: It is well known that Bill Monroe accompanied a black fiddler and guitarist named Arnold Shultz at dances in and around his hometown of Rosine, Kentucky. This is particularly significant in terms of black/white cultural interchange, for it points out not only the obvious—that Monroe learned much from Shultz that was later to be infused into the lonesome, bluesy side of bluegrass music, his creation, which is enjoying a tremendous renaissance of popularity today—it also means (and Monroe substantiates this)—that Shultz was playing square-dance music on the fiddle. His choice of notes may have been bluesy, but he was still playing what we'd call traditionally "white" tunes (for white audiences) like "Sally Goodin'."

And the list goes on: It is also well known that Hank Williams was profoundly influenced in his youth by a black street singer from Montgomery, Alabama, named Rufe Payne, known by both the townspeople and history as Tee-tot. And Jimmie Skinner, a singer popular in the late 1940s and early 1950s, recalls being drawn to the blues as a youth in rural central Kentucky as much because of the sound of the guitar as the emotive singing. And it is said that a black Kentuckian—Arnold Shultz—taught both Ike Everly and Mose Roger (who in turn influenced the legendary Merle Travis) to play the blues on the guitar in two-finger style, often called nigger-pickin', not in derision but in admiration.

If there's any lesson to be drawn from this, it's not, I think, a sociological one, not an abstract thesis about black/white relationships, about polarization and antagonisms, about civil rights nor cross-cultural bridges. It is simply that music in general (think of the great cross-cultural exchanges between white and black jazz musicians, far ahead of the rest of society) and the guitar in particular appealed to all, and, more importantly, the guitar was an instrument relatively easy to learn and simple to carry, whether to work or to a party.

Both blacks and whites sang the blues in the rural South in the early days of this century, for the blues are, above all, emotional expressions of the human heart, and the need for this expression is common to all humans, men or women, black or white. That they were easily played on an instrument with a voice so complementary to the feeling of the blues made a certainty of the success of the guitar in the early years of the century and allowed for the phenomenon of rural blues as a relatively colorblind musical form.

For example: Although there is ample evidence that there existed plentiful personal discrimination against him, certainly there was no musical discrimination against Deford Bailey, one of the best-loved figures of the Grand Ole Opry in its early years. A black harmonica player (another instrument well suited to blues expression), Bailey was popular both on the Opry and in personal appearances, although he usually was forced to board in a different part of town after completion of the road show. Still, it was his harmonica, not the color of his skin, that endeared him to Opry audiences and listeners.

Nor did the pioneer A&R men make much of a distinction in searching out rural blues. The early men who made field recordings, such as Ralph Peer, Frank Walker, and Art Satherley, headed departments for their companies that covered both race

The Jimmie Rodgers Entertainers in 1927. *Left to right*: Jack Grant, Jimmie Rodgers, Jack Price, and Claude Grant. It was this band who left Rodgers high and dry on the eve of their audition for Victor's Ralph Peer, changing their name to the Tenneva Ramblers and recording without him. (*Bob Pinson*)

(rural black) and hillbilly (rural white) music. Among Peer's numerous discoveries, for example, was Mamie Smith, whose success attracted national interest to the blues; and it was Satherley who first sought out and recorded the legendary Ma Rainey and Blind Lemon Jefferson. It is interesting that while the market outlets —the record stores and music shops and, later, jukeboxes—were largely segregated as to the availability of race and hillbilly recordings, the music was in many ways remarkably similar. The early records of Gene Autry and Jimmie Davis prove this, as, of course, do those of that legendary white bluesman Jimmie Rodgers.

Even Rodgers' most avid supporters wouldn't claim he was the first white man to sing the blues or to record them; it's just that it was he who, in the depths of the Depression, sold millions of Victor records, a great number of them (some quite risqué for the time) blues, often with an echoing yodel that was first his trademark and eventually an integral part of his public persona as "America's Blue Yodeler."

It would be natural at this point to list the country singers, both male and female, who were greatly influenced by Rodgers, but it is a futile exercise. Virtually every country singer has learned from an earlier singer, whether by record, radio, or in person, and no matter whose career you follow, it inevitably leads back to the direct influence of Rodgers or someone who in turn had been influenced by him. Certainly the simple recorded sound of his music has been the inspiration for uncounted aspiring singers and guitarists, many of whom began learning their craft long after Rodgers' untimely death in 1933.

Rodgers was, like so many before him, influenced in his musical style by black section hands and railroaders. His father, Aaron Rodgers, was a railroad man, and young Jimmie frequently hung out among the railroaders, both black and white, learning the lore of the rails as well as the powerful effects of music. In fact, he was taught by blacks to play the guitar and banjo during his years as a water boy and hanger-on. Rodgers himself took up a career in railroading as a teen-ager (hence the "Singing Brakeman" image), pursuing it until continued bouts with tuberculosis forced him to retire while still in his twenties. Although it is commonly thought that Rodgers took up music only as an alternative occupation once he was unable to continue working the rails, actually he had set his sights on a career as an entertainer long in advance of his retirement. But a professional musician's career in those days was not only a chancy, insecure, and often ill-paying venture (as it is today) but was also—as opposed to our current attitude of veneration toward musicians and artists in general—considered to be a somewhat low, unsavory, and suspect way to make a living. Apparently the security of railroading rather than its glamor kept Rodgers from trying a career as a singer before the decision was forced upon him.

Even when Rodgers' decision on a career was made, in his early efforts he was only occasionally successful in landing musical work. He surfaced crooning pop songs here, playing tenor banjo there, and even playing ukulele in a Hawaiian band for a time. In fact, on the eve of a tryout for Ralph Peer, who represented Victor Records in 1927, Rodgers' band dropped him, changed their name from the Jimmie Rodgers Entertainers to the Tenneva Ramblers, and were signed and recorded without him. Although dejected and more than a bit put out, he talked his way into a solo tryout for Peer, and although Peer was not particularly enthusiastic, he did agree to record Rodgers as a solo singer.

Rodgers' selections for the first recording session were a bit unusual, considering his lasting reputation as a blue yodeler. Rather than the lonesome, moaning yodel punctuating twelve-bar blues, which continue to characterize his blue-yodeling style, Rodgers chose to sing a crooning lullaby called "Sleep, Baby, Sleep" and a sentimental World War I ballad, "The Soldier's Sweetheart." The records sold well enough—but only barely well enough—to warrant another session, this time in Camden, New Jersey (Victor's home offices), and it was at that time that Rodgers recorded "T for Texas," a song that had an electrifying effect on record buyers throughout the southern states, and his record sales shot up dramatically. Before long he was Victor's best-selling singer, recording in addition to the blue yodels (such as "T for Texas") a strange but effective mixture of sentimental parlor songs, hobo songs, vaudeville tunes, and an occasional cowboy or even Hawaiian tune.

Rodgers' recording and full-time performing career lasted only six short years, until his death from tuberculosis in 1933. Although ill and weak, he and Victor were trying to make as many recordings as possible in their New York Studios before the inevitable end came, and the final recordings were finished only days before his death.

Rodgers' career was a pivotal one and in a great number of ways related to the course country music was to take for decades. He was, for example, the first country singer to establish himself firmly as a solo performer, both on record and in person. While he occasionally used a band on his personal appearances (of which he made all too few due to his increasingly fragile health) and on record, it was Rodgers as an individual, rather than as a band member or leader, who was in the forefront. His record labels in general add no "and his . . ." group name; he alone was the featured performer, and Rodgers was largely responsible for the development of this trait in country music, in striking contrast to the all-pervasive band concept so firmly entrenched in the country music of the era, regardless of region.

The phrase "to establish himself firmly" is carefully chosen in this context, for it is obvious that Vernon Dalhart's solo identity was established with his million-selling "The Prisoner's Song" in 1925—two years before Rodgers ever faced a recording microphone. Yet Dalhart, for some reason, didn't seem to feel that an identity as a recording artist—at least a recording artist of hillbilly songs—was terribly important, and he recorded for scores of different record labels under a bewildering variety of pseudonyms. It may well be that Dalhart, trained in light opera, shared with many of his fellow stage performers a disdain for recordings (which were, admittedly, of quite poor quality in the era of acoustic recording), considering them to have little professional status and viewing them as little more than an easy way to make a few dollars. Whatever his reasons, although it is quite possible that his voice was heard *more* on record than Rodgers', Dalhart never established the devoted following nor the strong identity that Rodgers did on record. Again, it was an attribute of Rodgers' career that was to have a tremendous effect on the ensuing history of country music.

Rodgers has had yet another remarkable effect that goes beyond the blues or even the yodel, which was to become so popular in country music during the 1940s. Historian Bill C. Malone, in *Country Music U.S.A.*, sees Rodgers' role as a pivotal one in the development of the American love affair with the singing cowboy in the two decades following the Singing Brakeman's death. More than his tremendous influence on young Gene Autry, who was to make a nationwide mania of "western" music and film within the following few years, Malone contends it was Rodgers' romantic view of the West as expressed in song that whetted the nation's hunger for such a phenomenon, adding the medium of song to a West already romanticized in print (in the ever-popular novels of Zane Grey) and on screen, for the western had been a popular film genre dating back to Edison's first major feature, "The Great Train Robbery," an action-packed, if brief, western thriller.

Rodgers' influence on up-and-coming country singers was felt immediately. By the time of his death his personal style had already become a musical style, emulated by many who were to become famous later with styles of their own. In fact, it seems that the American Record Company (ARC) signed Gene Autry on the strength of his singing style, which was at the time (1929–1930) indistinguishable from that of Rodgers. Autry's first records were either "covers" (similar versions by different artists on a competitive label) of Rodgers' hits or were blue yodels ("Bear Cat Papa Blues," "Do Right Daddy Blues," etc.) that might just as easily have been recorded

Jimmie Rodgers in cowboy dress. Some feel it was he who began the stylistic trend toward western music despite his solid identity as a Mississippi blue yodeler. (*Bob Pinson*)

by Rodgers in his own blue yodel series. Similarly, Montana Slim (Wilf Carter), Jimmie Davis, Hank Snow, Ernest Tubb, and scores of others began their careers as yodelers around the time of Rodgers' death, and the yodel even found its way into the thoroughly Appalachian sound of the Carter Family (such as in their haunting "Coal Miner's Blues") and the Monroe Brothers by the middle 1930s. A decade later it had become a staple in the repertoire of singing cowboys, bringing great success to noted yodelers Elton Britt, Rosalie Allen, Laura Lee McBride, Patsy Montana, Carolina Cotton, and Kenny Roberts. But by the 1940s most of the blue was out of the yodel, and vocal pyrotechnics rather than lonesome wails were more the order of the day.

Even though Rodgers was the most important and certainly the most famous early white bluesman, he was far from being the only one. Cliff Carlisle, later to achieve fame in a brother act with his younger sibling Bill, played accompaniment on several of Rodgers' recorded songs and was one of the first whites to explore the possibilities of the Hawaiian guitar played with a blues feel. The bluesy steel guitar uses a sound derived from the black "bottleneck" guitar style, a term derived from the broken-off neck of a whiskey bottle placed on the little finger of the left hand, producing the

Of the multitude of singers directly affected by Jimmie Rodgers, none has been so closely identified with him as Ernest Tubb, who later spearheaded the entirely different honky-tonk style. Tubb, here shown about 1940, before he joined the Opry, was so devoted to Rodgers that he became a friend, then a protégé, of his widow, Carrie Rodgers, who eventually gave him Rodgers' favorite guitar, a Martin 000–45, which Tubb treasures to this day. (*Bob Pinson*)

Cliff Carlisle, who was early to explore the blues possibilities inherent in the Hawaiian guitar. One of the pioneers of the instrument, he recorded several tunes with Jimmie Rodgers. Long retired from music, Carlisle now lives in Lexington, Kentucky, where he was a sign painter for many years. (*Country Music Foundation Library and Media Center*)

wailing slide that was particularly compatible with the feel of the blues both then and now. Johnny Winter, the Allman Brothers, and Eric Clapton, among many others, have used and popularized the technique in contemporary rock music.

At any rate, Carlisle, as opposed to bottleneck players, played the guitar in the traditional Hawaiian manner: seated, holding the guitar face up, flat on the lap, and fretting the raised strings with a steel bar. Carlisle's choice of notes, however, was far removed from that heard on sunbathed Pacific isles; it was far more redolent of red Georgia clay or black Mississippi bottomland, and it suited Rodgers' music perfectly. It hasn't been so very long ago since the Carlisle-type blues sound was once again popularized in country music—"Harper Valley PTA" or the increasingly bluesy use of the dobro in bluegrass music all owe a debt to that earlier style pioneered by Carlisle, Jimmy Tarlton, and Frankie Marvin.

The blues remained in country music throughout the 1930s but became increasingly diffused and directionless with the passing of Rodgers, the great exponent of the style. Nearly every country entertainer of the 1930s and 1940s featured a blues number or two on his or her show, but the earlier imitators, the Tubbs, Autrys, Snows, and Davises, all eventually went on to develop their own styles and had considerable success in new directions. An interesting exception to the rule was one of the great brother acts of the era, Alton and Rabon Delmore, who softened the blues for mountain ears with "Blues Stay Away from Me," yet introduced the white rural listeners to the driving eight-to-the-bar beat with "Freight Train Boogie." Although one would scarcely consider the Delmore Brothers a blues act, these two natives of north Alabama were able to help keep the blues tradition alive in country music while still performing in a classic southeastern style.

Riley Puckett, the famous blind guitarist whose imaginative use of bass runs gave rise to a whole style of country rhythm guitar playing. His singing was extremely black-influenced, and he even recorded a song, "Darkey's Wail" (actually "John Henry"), in the black "bottleneck" style. He introduces the song on record by saying, "I'm going to play for you this time a little piece which an old southern darkey I heard play, coming down Decatur Street the other day, called 'His Good Gal Done Throwed Him Down.' " (*Country Music Foundation Library and Media Center*)

Robert Lunn, "The Talking Blues Boy," who brought his venerable blues style to the Opry for two decades.

ROBERT LUNN

Another exponent of blues style, or more specifically *a* blues style, in country music's middle years was the Opry's Robert Lunn, "The Talking Blues Boy." Talking blues—hard-luck stories, occasionally quite risqué, narrated over a bluesy guitar accompaniment—was not a new form, having been pioneered on record by Chris Bouchillon and others in the 1920s. It was Lunn, however, a frequent part of Roy Acuff's road show, who kept the style alive long after its initial popularity had waned, and it was thus unfortunate that Lunn died just as urban folk groups such as the New Lost City Ramblers were reviving the talking blues and delighting both a new generation and a new audience with them. Similarly, the talking blues of Oklahoman Woody Guthrie had a powerful influence on folksong revivalists of the early 1960s and inspired countless protest-oriented talking blues such as "Talking Vietnam" by Tom Paxton. Phil Ochs and Bob Dylan also contributed to the genre. Jerry Reed might be considered a modern counterpart of Lunn, for he frequently comes close to a talking-blues style with novelty tunes like "When You're Hot, You're Hot" and "Alabama Wild Man." A crucial stylistic difference is Reed's manic black vocal style heard over his "hot" bluesy guitar, in contrast to the more traditional talking-blues style: a dry, deadpan, almost expressionless delivery that made the hard-luck stories seem all the harder by contrast. A good recent example of contemporary humor delivered in the traditional talking-blues style is Dick Feller's "Making the Best of a Bad Situation."

By the 1940s the segregation of black and white music was solidifying, stiffening, and despite Robert Lunn, the Delmore Brothers, and a few others, there were few indeed who emphasized blues on record or in person, other than through the obligatory inclusion of a tune or two in live performance. Throughout this decade it is certain that popular music gradually drew less from the deep well of rural blues

Jerry Reed, the "Alabama Wild Man," is popular in both country and popular music yet is the direct descendent of a long talking-blues tradition. (*Country Music Foundation Library and Media Center*)

and its musically sophisticated offspring, jazz, than it had during its love affair with jazz a decade or two earlier. The 1940s was an era of great change in country music, and as the string band was phased out in favor of the singing cowboy, so was the country blues eliminated as a style with an identity of its own.

Of course the death of Jimmie Rodgers and the artistic maturation of his imitators were partial causes of the decline in country blues, but beyond this the increasing urbanization of America, a process speeded up a thousandfold during World War II, forced blacks and whites together in situations of tension and division. Newly urbanized rural peoples of both races, caught up in the strangeness of urban and/or northern environments, tended to turn inward to their music for solace and comfort and thereby gained a strength of cultural identity from this thread of cultural continuity. The result: Black music became blacker, delving deeply into the agonizing blues of Muddy Waters and Howlin' Wolf; and white music became whiter, the crying steel guitar of Roy Wiggins behind Eddy Arnold's plaintive ballads giving transplanted rural whites a vision of their own identity, the lyrics of "Born to Lose" becoming an anthem for the displaced, homesick, confused rural white.

This, of course, is not to say that all was happy and peaceful and fulfilling in rural America, particularly in the South, in the years before World War II, that it was a place of sharing and caring and brotherhood. There can be little argument that it was not, for the most part, a happy time or place. But poor whites were as poor as poor blacks, and there was for a time a remarkable cross-cultural musical exchange that was lost—at least for a while—when the poor of both races left their farms and country towns for the cities.

At any rate, if the blues had been submerged and temporarily laid aside in the 1940s, their influence had changed country music unalterably, and if the rough edges of rural blues had been smoothed—even polished—to make them palatable to the country music audience, they were present nonetheless: in the "hot" solos of Bob Wills' fiddlers, guitarists, and horn men; in the "high, lonesome sound" of Bill Monroe's singing and the slurred phrasing of his fiddlers; in the rhythmic, syncopated, electrifying guitar picking of Merle Travis; and in the wailing tone and bent notes of Hank Williams' emotive voice. The blues didn't really go away; they were simply absorbed more deeply within country music's mainstream.

If anything, the increasing separation of musical styles—polarization, if you will—was accelerated in the early 1950s with the rise in popularity of a crude, powerful, gut-wrenching musical form that was only then beginning its development. With white audiences, the Ink Spots were just fine; they were safe. But the heavy beat and powerful, suggestive lyrics of Little Willie John were more than just a little dangerous, and as that type of music began to be heard more and more frequently, country music retreated more and more deeply into the "weeper," the cheatin' song, the honky-tonk genre.

This retreat from the music of black America couldn't go on indefinitely, of course: The cracks began to show when a white Pennsylvania leader of a local

The legendary Merle Travis. A great singer; one of the all-time great and influential guitarists; writer of "Sixteen Tons," "Dark as a Dungeon," "Nine-Pound Hammer," and other classics; and talented as well as a cartoonist and author—the man seems to have endless talents.

popular country band began incorporating some of this style into his performances, and the tremendous response from youth put Bill Haley and the Comets—and what was soon to be called rock and roll—on the map forever. Haley was quickly followed by a host of other aspiring country singers who felt the pulsating, rhythmic beat of this new black-rooted music as well as another beat, that of the pulse of American youth of all colors, and many of these artists would carve out enormous successes for themselves, the list headed, of course, by Elvis Presley.

This phenomenon will be traced in greater detail in chapter 10, but it is especially important to point out that neither the black blues player nor the white country singer gained much from the sudden explosion of rock and roll. In fact, both the "race" and "hillbilly" (by this time called rhythm and blues and country and western by music trade papers) record industries suffered a tremendous decline during the peak years of rock and roll. There were exceptions, of course: Fats Domino (whose "Blueberry Hill" was originally sung in a 1940 Gene Autry western) and Chuck Berry on one hand, Marty Robbins and Sonny James on the other. In general, however, it was the white city singer who experienced the greatest successes by watering down the rawness of black rock, and both the "R&B" and "C&W" industries struggled painfully with slumping record sales and declining audiences for personal appearances, as each musical form vied for a claim to Elvis and his imitators. It is interesting as a sidelight that rock and roll was such a confusing and powerful phenomenon that despite massive record sales, the "pop" departments of the major record labels were probably hurt worst of all: There was suddenly virtually no demand for the expensive crooners who had been their big sellers only a year or two before. It took the entire industry, not just "soul" and "country" as they are called today, a long time to recover psychologically, despite overall high revenues.

It's interesting, frustrating, and possibly pointless to speculate on just what it was about the climate or temper of the times that made the youth of the middle and late fifties, both black and white, urban and rural, respond to the strong blues influence so evident in rock and roll; what it was that united them in spirit with the youths and adults of the turn of the century who participated so freely and fully in roughly comparable cross-cultural musical exchanges. The phenomenon is part of a complex problem sociologists and historians have been grappling with ever since its occurence, but at least part of the answer may be as simple as Jimmie Skinner's recollection of his first introduction to the blues: The sound of the guitar (albeit electrified by the 1950s) in combination with the unsophisticated and ingenuous heartfelt lyrics of the blues proved to be a common denominator to which large numbers of people are drawn, regardless of age, race, or era. It was as true in 1957 as it was fifty years earlier; it is true today, although, musical fads being what they are, blues/country material has not retained the degree of popularity it reached in the 1950s. And, I suspect, it will be true fifty years from now, and fifty after that, as our interest in musical roots periodically recurrs.

At any rate, throughout the 1950s the blues influence in pure country music was negligible, even deliberately avoided, except where country singers would try for a "crossover" hit in the rock and roll field, or record a couple of rock or rocklike numbers to fill up an album. Still, this was merely an often-embarrassing concession to rock and roll as a stepchild rather than a homage to or recognition of the influence of rock and roll's fathering music, the blues.

What has come to be called rockabilly, the early music of Elvis, Carl Perkins, Buddy Holly, Johnny Cash, Bill Haley, Jerry Lee Lewis, Conway Twitty, and many many others, will be dealt with later; suffice it to say here that this music represented an attempt by young whites to genuinely perform and create rock, not merely emulate it. Yet the tradition that created "The Great Speckled Bird" and "Wreck on the Highway" left an unmistakable and ineradicable mark on the voices and the music of the rockabillies that the Philadelphia rockers, for example, never had, and later, with a new emergence of country music, many of the rockabillies of the 1950s were to return to their country roots.

Hints of the blues have begun to return to country music during the last few years, although largely as nostalgic reworkings rather than as new creations within the blues style. Merle Haggard's "California Blues" preceded and promoted his marvelous tribute album to Jimmie Rodgers, and Tom T. Hall's "The Year That Clayton Delaney Died" echoed much of Rodgers' sound for a reason: Hall deliberately used it to evoke an earlier era, to describe a local singer (obviously one of the thousands of Rodgers' imitators) Hall had known in his youth.

And of course the rock-and-roll songs of the 1950s, done in country style, keep appearing on the country charts, but these are meant to appeal to the listener in his or her late twenties or early thirties who remembers the selections nostalgically from youth, and the connection of these musical efforts with true country blues is far removed and tenuous at best.

Currently the musical styles of country and soul are as far apart as ever, maybe more so: Tammy Wynette's listeners have little interest in Roberta Flack; Stevie Wonder fans seldom seek out Buck Owens records. And the phenomenon of a Charlie Rich selling well in all markets (country, soul, pop, easy listening) simply proves what has always been true in American popular music: Good songs, good performances, combining innocuous hints of many musical styles but belonging in none, will possess broad-based appeal.

In an increasingly urbanized society it is difficult to predict whether this musical polarization will continue or whether a reunion of styles and tastes will occur at some point in the future. It remains a certainty, however, that regardless of varying musical sophistication, short-lived fads, or changing tastes, some portion of humankind will always be profoundly moved by the simple sound of the human voice, a guitar, and the blues.

Minnie Pearl, the 1975 addition to the Country Music Hall of Fame. (*Grease Brothers*)

4

COMEDY
"These Shoes Are Killing Me!"

Lonzo: Well where's Jody today?

Oscar: Didn't I tell you? We had a terrible accident while we were flying!

Lonzo: You did? What happened?

Oscar: Well I was practicing my stunt flying and done a few rolls and flips and Jody fell out of the plane!

Lonzo: That's terrible!

Oscar: Well, he had a parachute with him.

Lonzo: Well what a relief. That's good.

Oscar: No, that's bad! It didn't open.

Lonzo: That is bad!

Oscar: No, it's good. There was a haystack below him.

Lonzo: Oh, well that's good.

Oscar: No! That's bad! There was a pitchfork in the haystack!

Lonzo: That *is* bad!

Oscar: No, it was good 'cause he missed the pitchfork!

Lonzo: Oh, well that is good.

Oscar: Nope, it's bad. He missed the haystack, too.

Among scholars and historians surely the most-ignored aspect of country music, its performance, musicians, and entertainers, is humor. Many a tape, in fact, of live performances has been edited by devoted music lovers who snip out the usually corny and not always tasteful between-selection jokes and patter in order to preserve the purity of the musical performance. Yet to the average fan of the 1930s and 1940s, the jokes, the skits, the blackface or rube act were as likely as not the most vivid, the most memorable part of the show. And even today, although humor of late has been rather neglected, frequently the most striking moments of a package show are those spent with Minnie Pearl or Jerry Clower, rather than with the honey-voiced crooner who was the drawing card.

Max Terhune and Little Elmer. Terhune, an alumnus of the National Barn Dance, was featured in countless B-westerns. Truth to tell, he wasn't all that great as a ventriloquist, but he was tremendously funny. This photo dates from 1937. (*Country Music Foundation Library and Media Center*)

One of the most popular comedians of the 1930s and 1940s was Cousin Emmy, who first brought the song "Ruby" to national attention.

Although it is true that comedy is probably performed less frequently now than ever before, it has always played a large part in country performance, at least in professional performance. In fact, music and comedy were inseparable from the start—a start that goes back beyond vaudeville and the theater circuits; a start that provided Roy Acuff, Bob Wills, Gene Autry, and many others with their first professional experience: the medicine show.

Long before the turn of the century, enterprising practitioners of medical arts of dubious quality discovered that nostrums and cure-alls, usually heavily laced with alcohol, sold well to the isolated peoples of the flat prairies or the Appalachian foothills, regions where contact with cities, real doctors, and genuine medicine were infrequent at best. These entrepreneurs also discovered that the fastest way to draw a crowd to a wagon was to have a musician or two on the tailgate of the wagon, fiddling a lively tune. These musicians often doubled, by force of circumstance, as actors and comedians who put on humorous plays and skits, often in blackface, hoping to retain whatever crowds the music had attracted before the good "doctor" commenced his pitch. Once his oratorical powers had interested the crowd in his potion, the musicians/comedians/actors took on yet another duty: hawking the bottles to the audience. The medicine-show circuit provided a strange, nomadic life, although perhaps no stranger, comparatively, than the lives country musicians were to live in years to come.

The lifestyle—the seedy hotels, the flashy, worldly "show people," the living out of suitcases on endless tour—was the reason that a career as a professional musician was held in such low esteem for so long among rural Americans. It is understandable that an entertainer's association with the generally disreputable (although exciting) medicine show caused many rural parents to dissuade their sons from such a career. Yet many a musically talented farm or ranch youth was to take up this unsavory, nomadic existence in preference to years of grinding toil on the land.

For example: Felled by sunstroke, Roy Acuff was forced to give up his chosen career of baseball and practiced his fiddle while recuperating. Overheard by a "med-show" operator named Dr. Hauer, Acuff took the chance (he was assured he'd only have to fiddle at night) and went with Hauer's show on tours through Appalachia and the Deep South. Similarly, young Gene Autry ran away from his Oklahoma ranch to join the Fields Brothers Marvellous Medicine Show. With such experience behind them, it is no accident that both these men incorporated extensive and virtually nonstop comedy routines into their stage shows when their popularity peaked in the 1940s. Acuff has repeatedly stated that every member of his band was expected to be a comedian as well as a musician, and Autry, in addition to forming a cast that included a well-known standup comedian (Smiley Burnette or, later, Pat Buttram) and a midget who did comedy and rope tricks, also assigned various gags among his band members and did his own comedy routines, with Johnny Bond as straight man. Young Bob Wills also ran off on a medicine show at least twice as a youth, playing the fiddle and doing blackface comedy. His show, at its peak in the 1930s and 1940s, did not include comedy, because the Texas Playboys was first and

Smiley Burnette was Gene Autry's radio and film sidekick for years, portraying Frog Millhouse. He was actually an extremely talented and versatile musician, a fact he was fairly careful not to let on. To the *right*, with guitar, is a young Merle Travis, and seated at the far *right* is Charles Starrett, star of this 1945 film, *Roaring Rangers*. (*National Screen Service Corp.*)

last a dance band. His medicine-show training revealed itself more subtly: in the fact that the dance itself never stopped, and in the sharp humor of his witty onstage asides.

If the medicine show was one proving ground for country musicians and entertainers, yet another, slightly later, was vaudeville. Although generally associated with the New York stage rather than the Opry stage, a number of country musicians and comedians got their start with these traveling shows, for the part of the rube and/or blackface comedian was ever popular in the small towns of the Midwest and South. In fact, in the 1930s, as vaudeville was itself fading (losing its head-to-head battle with motion pictures for dominance in theaters) and radio barn dances such as the Opry were flourishing, many of these barn dances used ex-vaudeville talent to shore up their roster of comedians.

Steel guitarist, actor, songwriter, comedian, Frankie Marvin
was from the old school that believed you should do it all.
Popular in vaudeville, he is best known for his steel-guitar work
with Gene Autry. (*Frankie Marvin*)

An early photo of Benjamin Whitey Ford (the "Duke of Paducah") and Frankie Marvin, who teamed up in the late 1920s as Ralph and Elmer. Ford later rose to great heights as a comedian, having his own network radio show, a syndicated newspaper column, and a spot on the Opry's network program. He is still active and busy today, entertaining at dinners and conventions across the country. (*Frankie Marvin*)

In its heyday vaudeville stretched nationwide, its performers traveling on various "circuits" for various companies. And although it was mostly country comedians—like Jamup and Honey and the Duke of Paducah—who thrived in vaudeville, country singers also made the tours occasionally: Jimmie Rodgers, for instance, toured with Swain's Hollywood Follies for a time, and even as severely traditional an Opry string band as Uncle Dave Macon and Sam and Kirk McGee took several tours together on the Keith-Orpheum circuit. Although, like the medicine show before it, vaudeville was considered all too worldly and unsavory by many of the God-fearing men and women who worked the land, at least it paid a great deal better than the med show—a consolation (and inducement) to the performer, if not to his distraught relatives.

Country-oriented comedy which filtered down from both the med show and vaudeville traditions tended to fall into two rough categories: blackface and rube, either done solo or with a straight man. Actually, except for the phony Negro accent and black makeup, the humor and jokes of both blackface and rube comedy were just about the same: self-deprecatory—but ultimately affectionate—jibes at the ignorance of the "country boy." Be he black or white, there was often a straight man who was, like the audience, well aware of the mental shortcomings of the rube. An old Lasses and Honey blackface routine clearly evidences this:

> Honey: Say listen here, Lasses, I supppose you heard 'bout me gitting all tied up and bound down last summer with them bounds of matrimonial bliss and blisters, din't you? Well I'm sick of my deal already.
> Lasses: Well Honey, you know the course of true love never runs smooth! By the way, wasn't your wife's maiden name Berger?
> Honey: Yes sir! Her name used to be Berger, and she's got two brothers, Ham and Limb.
> Lasses: Appropriate names!
> Honey: I'll say they is! And Ham and Limb are in the iron and steel business.
> Lasses: Your wife's brothers are in the iron and steel business?
> Honey: Yeah. One of 'em irons clothes and the other steals 'em!
> Lasses: Some family! You know, speaking of marriages, my younger brother that ran away from home three years ago is now happily married with a big family.
> Honey: You don't mean to tell me!
> Lasses: Yep, I certainly do, Honey. And it's a very peculiar thing about my brother and his wife, too. Their first two years of married life were spent in Twin Falls, Idaho, and while living there his wife presented him with twins.
> Honey: You don't mean it!
> Lasses: Oh yes I do! And then they moved from Twin Falls to Three Rivers, Michigan, and we just had a wire yesterday that his wife presented him with triplets!

Honey: You don't mean to tell me!
Lasses: Sure do! Say, what're you laughing at, Honey?
Honey: Why I was just laughing about it's a good thing your brother and his wife didn't move up in Canada to them Thousand Islands!

On the other hand, many performers preferred to work alone, frequently relying on their character's attempted canniness, which they are never able to sustain to achieve their goal, as the basis of their humor. Minnie Pearl is a master of this style, as was longtime radio favorite the Duke Of Paducah, whose "Let me on the wagon, boys, these shoes are killin' me!" was as famous in its day as is Minnie Pearl's "Howdeee! I'm just so proud to be here!" Here's a sample of one of the Duke's monologues:

There comes a time in every man's life when he sits down, thinks over all the mistakes he has made, shakes his head sadly, and wishes he was young enough to make 'em all over again.

When I was younger, I used to take long walks in the spring with pretty girls. And I used to carve our initials in the trees. Before I got married I had my initials carved in so many trees I used to get fan mail from woodpeckers.

Lonzo (*right*) and Oscar, one of the most popular acts on the Opry for years. They played the rube act to the hilt. (*Country Music Foundation Library and Media Center*)

The Louvin Brothers in 1946, at the start of their career. Superimposed on the photo of the brothers, Ira and Charlie, is Sal Skinner, a comedy character created by Ira, the mandolinist, and performed on stage shows. (*Charlie Louvin*)

Pat Buttram, a National Barn Dance alumnus, was Gene Autry's longtime radio sidekick. (*Country Music Foundation Library and Media Center*)

Occasionally a country singer takes on a whole alter ego: Ferlin Husky's character Simon Crum recorded and performed "on his own." (*Capitol Records*)

And I don't know whether the girls I went out with had will power or not—but they sure did have won't power!

All the women then tried to have hourglass figures; and a lot of them looked as if the sand had all run into the bottom of the glass!

When I was courting my fat wife, she tried to make herself look thin by lacing herself up tight when we went out. One day, I dropped around to see her when she wasn't expecting me, and she wasn't laced up. I was sure surprised to see her home front!

Of course I made a good match when I married and settled down. My wife was really prominent in Washington, Chicago, New York, and around the hips.

My wife said to me "You're always trying to get something for nothing! Don't you realize that hard work never hurt anybody?" I said "Yeah, I realize that, and I don't want to take any chances on spoiling its record!"

Anyway, I decided to get in on the war effort. The marines had a great deal cooked up before they found out I was too old: they were going to send me ashore with the first wave in beachhead landings to give the enemy false confidence! But the first wave objected so I ended up with a whack.

Anyway, my big fat wife decided to get in on the war effort, and so she decided to join the Wacs but was turned down absolutely. They said she was two inches too short for a hippopotamus her age.

So next she tried to enlist in the navy. The recruiting officer looked her over and said "Yeah, we need Waves, but not tidal waves!"

There's a lot of talk around today about war brides. My wife was a war bride. The day she became a bride the war started.

But you know, a lot of marriages these days wind up in the divorce courts and the fellow has to pay alimony. I don't believe in alimony—it's too much like buying hay for a dead horse.[*]

All this was to have a tremendous impact on the live country show, for, in imitation of the slicker acts that came to local theaters, country musicians of the area added comedy to the show they performed at the local schoolhouse. Even such traditional and heavily music-oriented old-time country groups as Mainer's Mountaineers, the Blue Sky Boys, and Bill Monroe had elaborate and hilarious comedy routines as regular parts of their stage shows.

It is just because country performance existed primarily in a live context that comedy is so little considered or remembered today, for as later generations have come to discover and explore country music, their focus has been on records, the only tangible evidence of what early country music performance was actually like. The ephemeral stage show is gone as soon as the curtain closes, and with it the gags, the jokes, the routines that were as much a part of it as were the songs. Yet it is the songs and singers we remember, revere, and study, while the laughter that filled the tent, the schoolroom, the auditorium, the theater, the barn passes from memory, even as similar versions of the songs are preserved in plastic and on tape for future generations.

[*] Benjamin F. Ford (The Duke of Paducah), *These Shoes Are Killin' Me* (New York: Radco Publishers, 1947), pp. 47–55. © copyright 1947 by Benjamin F. Ford. Used by permission.

Lasses and Honey, the most popular of the Opry blackface comedians in the early 1930s. (*Country Music Foundation Library and Media Center*)

Mainer's Mountaineers in a wild blackface skit in the middle 1930s, typical of their elaborate onstage antics. J.E., with the fiddle, and Wade, kneeling, are on the far *left*. Each Mainer brother later fronted a popular old-time country band of his own. (*Wade Marner*)

Despite his stern public image, Bill Monroe actually has a marvelous sense of humor and used to feature comic skits frequently with his Blue Grass Boys. In a rare photo (ca. 1943) of him smiling, Monore "pays off" Stringbean on the *left* and Bijou on the right. (*Howdy Forrester*)

Stringbean and Bijou out of blackface in their standard comedian's outfits, about 1944. (*Howdy Forrester*)

It is true that there are a few early comedy recordings: Gid Tanner's "Corn Likker Still in Georgia," the reenactment of a moonshiner's life, is a classic comedy disc. But the accent on comedy in country music performance is as much visual as aural, and few elaborate skits could be presented on record with any meaning.

Because of this, because records and a few rare films are our only link with the music's past, the role, status, and memory of the comedian has been, with a few outstanding exceptions, largely ignored. Yet during the years of country music's first recordings and of its first popularity on radio, comedy was already an integral part of nearly every professional band's stage show. Recordings and radio caused an explosion in country music's popularity, but the opportunity for professional achievement on the part of some musicians made them shoulder a responsibility to provide their audience with entertainment of a broader range than musical. So at that time comedy was an essential part of nearly every band's act—it was expected by the audience, and it was delivered.

As country music became a recognizable factor in American life, a "star" system began to develop. The transition from string bands to Roy Acuff, Bill Monroe, and Ernest Tubb completed in the years immediately preceding (1938–1943) demonstrates the growth of an Opry star system clearly. Similarly, a star system began to develop among comedians, and Smiley Burnette became a familiar face on the screen, the Duke of Paducah a familiar voice on radio, and Minnie Pearl a familiar fixture of Grand Ole Opry radio and road shows. Before long each major act on the Opry (or any of the barn dances, for that matter) tried always to carry a "star" comedian on road shows, although a comedian/band member (usually the bassist) was also frequently used for comic relief, a tradition that survives in the person of Speck Rhodes, who works with Porter Wagoner's show.

Sarie (*left*) and Sallie were one of the most popular comic duets on the Opry, all the more unusual in that they were women. With them are Sam and Kirk McGee, two other Opry pioneers. (*Bob Pinson*)

Even the Light Crust Doughboys got zany at times. W. Lee O'Daniel, at the mike, is not too out of place, but a teen-aged Leon McAuliffe (far *right*) makes a pretty strange hula girl.

Superb musicians as well as superb parodists, Homer (*right*) and Jethro had played together since their teens, finally making Chicago a home base. Jethro (Burns) has carried on a solo career since Homer's (Haynes) recent death. (*RCA Records*)

The growth of comedy stars was certainly encouraged by the recordings of Homer and Jethro, who, with extremely clever parodies of hit songs of the day, brought a cerebral and inventive aspect to country music humor. But even their work became predictable in time, though certainly no other comedian or comedy team—and many have tried—ever approached the consistent success enjoyed by Homer and Jethro in this limited recording style. The humorous "answer" record has really been the only effective use of comedy on records, although, of course, hundreds of "cute" songs (like Merle Travis' "Fat Gal") have been recorded from the fledgling days of commercial recording to the present.

Outside the narrow field of comedy recording, the star system in country comedy was further bolstered by the advent and development of package shows in the 1950s. The theory of the package show was simple: Rather than have Hank Snow play the high-school gym, utilize a half-dozen acts approaching Snow's popularity to fill the municipal auditorium of a major city. But while the package show was a boon to the careers of Lonzo and Oscar, Grandpa Jones, Minnie Pearl, Rod Brasfield, and a few others, it was a bane to the baggy-pants bass player, for it made it unnecessary to have a comedian in each band.

The package show as an institution is thought to have caused some serious damage to small acts, that is, to up-and-coming singers and bands who were not included in these all-star packages and therefore had difficulty obtaining the exposure necessary to maintain or develop a career. But nowhere was this negative

Two great comedian–banjo players of the Opry of the 1940s: Uncle Dave Macon and Cousin Rachel Veach. On guitar is Macon's son and longtime accompanist Dorris. (*Country Music Foundation Library and Media Center*)

Louis Jones came up with his character of Grandpa while still in his twenties; a listener, hearing him over an Akron radio station, wrote in asking his his age, saying "you sound like an old man." Jones toured with Bradley Kincaid and pioneered in country music television but has really come into his own in the past few years with the success of television's "Hee Haw." (*Grease Brothers*)

Speck Rhodes in the Opry dressing room. He is one of the few bass player/comedians who carries on a tradition that was once nearly universal. (*Grease Brothers*)

Rod Brasfield, one of the funniest men in country music's history. He rose from medicine shows to the Opry and was closely associated with Minnie Pearl, who developed the character she is famous for while a student at a fashionable Nashville finishing school. This photo was taken in the early 1950s. (*Country Music Foundation Library and Media Center*)

Clell Summey came to the Opry as Roy Acuff's dobro player in 1938, then branched out into the comedy team of Odie and Jody before settling on the character of the toothless Cousin Jody, whose wild steel-guitar (which he called his "biscuit board") version of "Listen to the Mockingbird" never failed to arouse an Opry audience. (*Country Music Foundation Library and Media Center*)

Mel Tillis, a superb songwriter, singer, and actor, who also happens to be a superb comedian. He had the courage and the ability to turn a natural stutter into a marvelous comic vehicle without any trace of self-pity. (*Grease Brothers*)

Archie Campbell came out of Knoxville, Tennessee, to achieve popularity as a comedian (and occasionally a singer) on the Opry and later on "Hee Haw," which he also helps script. Typical of today's non-slapstick comedians, his humor is both verbal and somewhat subtle, and his mixed-up versions of fairy tales like "Rindercella" are classics. (*Grease Brothers*)

Jerry Clower spent years entertaining friends, business contacts, and occasional conventions of fellow fertilizer salesmen with his broadly told and thickly accented tales of life in Yazoo, Mississippi. He now tells the same tales to appreciative audiences across the country on personal tours and on the Grand Ole Opry. (*Grease Brothers*)

The tragic double slaying of David Akeman and his wife, Estelle, lent a brutal and somber final note to what was otherwise a happy career, one that was actually on the rise thanks to the success of "Hee Haw." Quiet and reserved, Stringbean was genuinely loved by the musicians and entertainers he worked with. He has left a legacy of fine old-time music and comedy on record.

impact felt more than among comedians: The twenty minutes allotted each "star" on a package show barely allowed him time to introduce the band, sing a medley of his greatest hits, and sing the latest release, much less put on a long, involved comedy routine. Besides, as more than one singer/bandleader has put it, why pay to bring along your own comedian, or to have an "extra" band member, when there will be an Archie Campbell or Don Bowman on the show to do nothing but comedy (these days consisting of monologues and songs; skits seem to have disappeared forever) for his twenty minutes on stage.

So, through recent history, comedy has become less and less a part of country music, both on record and especially in performance, although in fairness it must be noted that the syndicated television favorite "Hee Haw" has revived a great number of the old skits and routines and much of the feeling of old-fashioned country humor. The style of the entire program, in fact, is rather like the Roy Acuff tent shows of thirty-five years ago: a mixture of broad humor, serious songs, slapstick, hymns, strangely dressed musicians/comedians, and a combination of old-time and more modern music.

The cast of "Hee Haw." Carrying on the tradition of country comedy.

Yet ultimately the growth of country music's suburban audience indicates that in all probability the broad stage hijinks of the past will never return. Love songs will be with the human race until it grinds to a halt, but for far too many of country music's listeners, the corny, exaggerated humor that was so much a part of country music entertainment in the past is too reminiscent of a background they seek to escape. Such comedy is, on the other hand, usually too alien and coarse to the ears of the urban northerner who seeks in country music purity and honest expression of feeling.

So the comedy routine, skit, and act are probably less likely than any other form of country music to enjoy a renaissance. That kind of comedy is too linked to a time and a way of life that are daily becoming history, and, as with all good things whose time has passed, there is little to be done but treasure the few available memories of its days of glory.

5
SINGING COWBOYS
"Back in the Saddle Again"

Of all the experiences of American life, one of the few that cuts across boundaries of age, social status, race, or location is that of sitting in a hushed movie theater on Saturday afternoon, accompanying the crack of six-guns with the rhythmic chewing of stale popcorn while staring wide-eyed at some handsome cowpuncher as he either roughs up a scurrilous scoundrel or two or leaps from a thundering stallion on to a fast-moving freight or rampaging stagecoach. If that rich and redolent experience was somehow missed, surely there is no one who has not been at least aware of the heroics of Matt Dillon on "Gunsmoke" or of the Cartwrights on "Bonanza," two longtime staples of television. Perhaps no occupations have been more glamorized over the years than those of cowboy, rancher, frontiersman, prospector, and prairie lawman. The romantic view of a cowboy's life as filled with danger, heroism, and courage is a national legend and legacy, part of us all. It is a delightful myth we know to be a myth, one that our grandfathers helped create, one that we continue to preserve.

Yet today positive sentiments toward the halcyon years of the western film seem to be scarce: Historians of western film look upon the whole genre of singing cowboys as an unhappy and unfortunate bastardization that diluted the purity of the classic action western, while historians of music, in general, tend to regard the genre with equal horror as a bastardization that not only diluted the purity of old-time country music but also bathed it in such gaudy commercialism that the music was stripped of its inherent dignity.

Pity the poor singing cowboy: denigrated and, except for a few diehards, forgotten. Yet he has filled an extremely influential role within country music (as well as, indeed, American life) that has largely been overlooked and ignored, for the singing cowboy, far from stripping dignity from old-time music, actually lent dignity and respect to a music that had been condescendingly known as "hillbilly" for years. Country music's contact with the singing western gave it the prestige and

Gene Autry in his peak years, ca. 1940. Here he was riding the heights of his enormous record successes. ("Be Honest with Me," "Tweedle-O-Twill," "South of the Border," and many others), his unprecedented popularity as a film star, the public reception to his Gene Autry Rodeo, and his newly launched "Melody Ranch" radio program. World War II was to seriously disrupt this happy pattern, as it did for millions of Americans. (*Gene Autry*)

Otto Gray (*left*) and his Oklahoma Cowboys were one of the first bands to bring country music to the Northeast and were extremely influential in determining what kind of country music was accepted and enjoyed in New England.

respectability it needed to enter the mainstream of American consciousness and to rise eventually to its current popularity. No matter what your favorite subgenre—bluegrass, western swing, Cajun—it might well have come to nothing more than an interesting historical footnote had not Gene Autry and the hoards of singing cowboys who followed him made a respectable profession of the country and/or western singer on a grand scale across the country and much of the world as well. It is, after all, out of the interest in and respect for the cowboy song that the possibility for deeper study of other facets of earthy, rural music arose.

Cowboy songs, of course, predated singing cowboys of the silver screen by decades and represent by themselves unique and fascinating documents of a place and a time in American history. The 1880s—the days of the flourishing cattle business and vast unfenced ranges—proved the initial era of the creation and spread of cowboy songs, though of course many of these songs originated even earlier. The words of the songs, usually taken from poems published in small local newspapers, pamphlets, or books, were put to the tune of some Irish or English melody the cowboys—usually immigrants from the East—already knew. More often than not their melodic repertoire was limited, and it is said that most of the classic songs of the cowboy were sung to only three or four basic tunes.

Contrary to the popular image of the cowboy riding the range with his ever-present guitar strapped to his side or over his shoulder, these early songs were usually sung without accompaniment, for the guitar was as late in reaching the Southwest as it had been in the Southeast. Once the guitar did appear, however, at about the turn of the century, the cowboys adopted it as quickly as had the folk musicians of the Southeast and for the same reasons: It was compact and provided sympathetic accompaniment to the human voice.

The Girls of the Golden West: Dorothy (Dolly—*left*) and Mildred (Millie) Good. A fine and popular cowgirl duet, their harmony yodels were harbingers of the trick yodeling to come in cowboy music. Pee Wee King admits having named his Golden West Cowboys in undisguised admiration of the talents of the charming Good sisters.

A 1928 publicity shot of the Musical Massey Family, who became better known in later years as Louise Massey and the Westerners, famous for "My Adobe Hacienda." They are (*left to right*) Dad Massey, Allen, Louise, Curt, and Milt Mabie (Louise's husband).

Carl T. Sprague first got the idea to record for Victor after hearing Vernon Dalhart's "The Prisoner's Song," and just missed having a million seller himself with "When the Work's All Done This Fall." This section of an early Victor catalog shows his repertoire to have been exclusively cowboy.

Southern Melody Soft Shoe Dance   Jimmy Smith
Mountain Blues   *Jimmy Smith* 20020

SOUTHERN RAILROAD QUARTET—Male Quartet
God Is Love   V-40002   Life's Railway to Heaven   V-40002

Spanish Merchant's Daughter   Stoneman Family   V-
Too Late   with Vocal Refrain   *Stoneman Family* 40206

SPRAGUE, CARL T.—Tenor with Guitar

Bad Companions	19747	If Your Saddle Is Good	V-40066
Boston Burglar	20534	Last Great Round Up	20932
Cowboy	21402	Last Longhorn	V-40197
Cowboy Love Song	20067	Mormon Cowboy	V-40246
Cowboy's Dream	20122	Oh Bury Me Not on Prairie	20122
Cowboy's Medi-		Rounded Up in Glory	20932
tation	V-40197	Two Soldiers	21194
Cowman's Prayer	21402	Utah Carroll	21194
Following Cow Trail	20067	Wayward Daughter	V-40246
Gambler	20534	When the Work's	
Here's to the Texas		All Done	19747
Ranger	V-40066		

Carl T. Sprague

STAMPS, FRANK, AND HIS ALL STAR QUARTET—with Piano

Because I Love Him	V-40090
Bringing in the Sheaves	21035
Come to the Savior	V-40062
Do Your Best	V-40122
Give the World a Smile	21072
Heavenly Chorus	V-40029

But cowboy songs, even when accompanied, were seldom sung as entertainment, but generally served as a relief from the pounding monotony and boredom of range work, as well as providing a way of quieting cattle to the solitary cowboy riding herd at night. The silvery yodels of a Roy Rogers are thus hardly representative of the singing capabilities of authentic cowboys. Scholar Fred G. Hoeptner in his liner notes to "Authentic Cowboys and Their Western Songs," quotes a writer of the era as saying, "I never did hear a cowboy with a real good voice. If he ever had one to start with, he lost it bawling at cattle."

Still, a song does not need to be polished to have meaning to a singer, and the rough-hewn cowboys quickly cast in song tales of stampedes and of tragic death on the prairie like "Utah Carroll" and "Little Joe the Wrangler." Such ballads are sentimental yet true to life, and many of these songs passed straight from newsprint into oral, or folk, tradition.,

Considering the romance that has surrounded the cowboy and the cowboy's life since the late nineteenth century, it is no wonder that commercial record companies tried to tap this rich wellspring of cowboy songs. In fact, shortly after recording Vernon Dalhart's "The Prisoner's Song" in New York, Victor Records recorded another native Texan, Carl T. Sprague, who had a substantial hit of his own, a near-million seller called "When the Work's All Done This Fall." Sprague, Jules Verne Allen, "Haywire Mac" McClintock, and others were rather busy, in fact, recording cowboy classics like "The Zebra Dun," "The Old Chisholm Trail," and "The Strawberry Roan" during phonograph records' big pre-Depression boom period, and the tradition of the singing cowboy—replete with guitar, which had been integrated into the folk tradition by then—was firmly fixed in the public mind by these descriptive, colorful ballads of a romantic, sometimes dangerous, often tedious life on the range.

It was perhaps inevitable that the film industry, which had traded upon the romanticism of the cowboy and the West from its beginning, would turn to cowboy songs to enrich the screen western. Apparently, however. the drawing power of western song was just not needed until the Depression, when for the first time public interest in western films began to wane. Although Ken Maynard, as early as 1930, occasionally took his guitar aside in a film or two to sing a song, it was not until 1934 that the concept of the singing-cowboy film as a genre, in which music was just as important as action (the industry euphemism then as now, for fist fights, gun battles, and high-speed chases), was developed and implemented by Herbert J. Yates and Nat Levine of Republic Studios.

It is said that in auditioning the part of the first singing cowboy, Levine screened actors who could sing but couldn't ride and actors who could ride but couldn't sing before finally deciding on a singer who could ride but couldn't act: a young yodeler from the National Barn Dance named Gene Autry. Autry had hit Hollywood riding high off the success of a recent hit record, a song he'd written with his sometimes partner Jimmy Long in the sentimental old-time mountain tradition called "That Silver Haired Daddy of Mine."

An authentic cowboy who once competed at the Calgary Stampede (as a calf roper, not a singer), Wilf Carter—usually known as Montana Slim—was and is a big favorite among northeastern and Canadian audiences. (*Country Music Foundation Library and Media Center*)

Yates and Levine first tried this handsome blond hillbilly singer with all those teeth in a Ken Maynard film in 1934, called "In Old Santa Fe" and the public response was so overwhelming that within three short years Autry was among Hollywood's top money-makers, inspiring a legion of imitators—many of whom were to become extremely important in country music themselves—and simultaneously impressing a whole generation, maybe two, with the meaning and worth of heartfelt country songs.

Autry was as authentic a cowboy as any born in the relatively late year of 1907, for he was born on a cattle farm near Tioga, Texas, and raised on a similar spread near Ravia, Oklahoma. Although as a teenager, he aspired to alternate vocals with saxophone solos, Autry joined the Field Brothers Marvellous Medicine Show while

Ken Maynard, one of the most popular of the film cowboys in the early talking period. Although as early as 1930 Maynard played or sang a tune or two on film, music was incidental to action, and he was really more of a cowboy who sang than a singing cowboy.

still in high school, apparently longing for a career as a professional singer both then and after graduation despite being forced to make a living as a telegrapher at a distant outpost for the St. Louis & Frisco Railroad. He found his way to New York—then the hub of the recording world—more than once, however, to audition for record companies; sometimes successfully, sometimes not. A connection with the American Record Company eventually led to success, and it was at this time that his style matured from what had been a letter-perfect imitation of Jimmie Rodgers to a warmer, mellower, more nasal tone, full of guileless sincerity, more like the voice we associate with those dark movie theaters on long-ago Saturday afternoons. After a brief stint at KVOO in Tulsa—Bob Wills' home station for eight years—he joined the WLS National Barn Dance in Chicago, and became one of the Midwest's most popular singers with his Conqueror Record Time program on WLS. His place in country music was assured with the resounding success of "That Silver Haired Daddy of Mine," but it was at this time, 1934, that he was called to Hollywood and the explosive popularity of singing cowboys was touched off.

OKLAHOMA'S YODELING COWBOY—GENE AUTRY

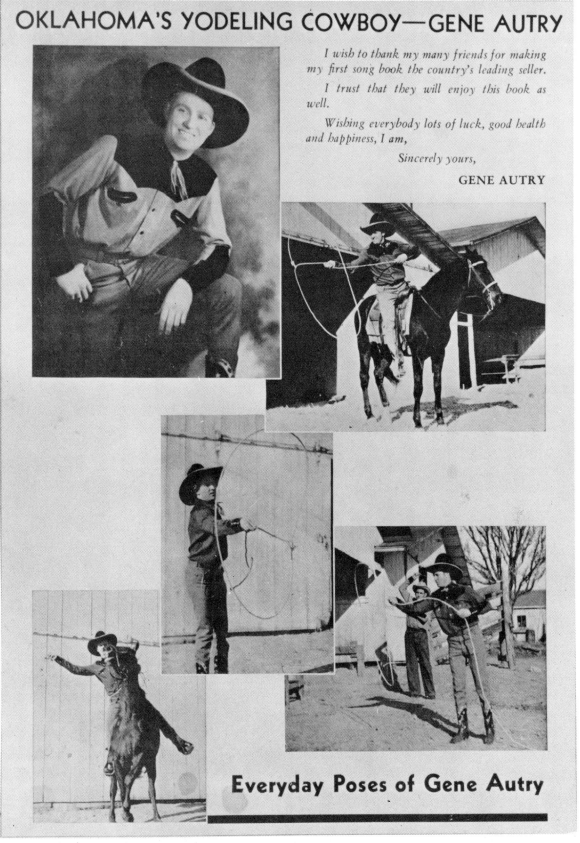

I wish to thank my many friends for making my first song book the country's leading seller.

I trust that they will enjoy this book as well.

Wishing everybody lots of luck, good health and happiness, I am,

Sincerely yours,

GENE AUTRY

Everyday Poses of Gene Autry

Gene Autry in his WLS days as "Oklahoma's Yodeling Cowboy." He'd done enough cattle ranching in his youth to know his way around a lariat and a horse, and this and his warm, sincere, unaffected singing voice made up for his deficiencies as an actor when Republic went looking for a singing cowboy.

Autry's popularity was, as one might suspect, not unnoticed by competing movie studios, and by 1936 two singing cowboys from the WHN Barn Dance in New York City found themselves in movies: Tex Ritter, who truly has become, both in film and on record, in the words of a recent album title, "An American Legend"; and Ray Whitley, who won renown as a songwriter although he was never able to rise above supporting roles as a singing sidekick in full-length westerns (although the RKO shorts he starred in are classics). Ritter and Whitley were followed by Dick Foran, and then two former members of Autry's vocal backup group: Broadway-voiced Eddie Dean, and Jimmy Wakely, later a big record seller on Capitol. In the late 1930s Republic Studios pulled a handsome singer from the established vocal group

Tex Ritter and White Flash. A law-school graduate who performed in several Broadway musicals, Ritter was also an authentic cowboy and a deep student of cowboy life and lore. Unsuccessful on record in his early career, he helped put newly founded Capitol Records on its feet in the early 1940s with hits like "There's a New Moon over My Shoulder" and "Have I Stayed Away Too Long? (*Country Music Foundation Library and Media Center*)

Ray Whitley, one of the earliest singing cowboys to follow Autry to the screen. Author of "Back in the Saddle Again" and several other western classics, he also helped Gibson design their SJ-200 guitar (the prototype of which is shown here), which became the sine qua non of country singers in the decades to follow.

the Sons of the Pioneers, changed his name from Len Slye to Roy Rogers, and thrust him into starring roles during a contract dispute with Autry; his first film, *Under Western Stars*, was initially scheduled as an Autry release. Rogers, of course, proved equal to the task, and has remained one of the most consistently successful entertainers in the world of show business: His recent hit recording, the nostalgia-oriented "Hoppy, Gene, and Me," proves he still has some muscle when it comes to record sales. Relative latecomers were Monte Hale and Rex Allen, another singer who, like Autry, was plucked from the stage of the National Barn Dance. Allen had the distinction of making the last of the singing-cowboy films *Down Laredo Way* in the middle 1950s. Autry's farewell film, aptly-titled *Last of the Pony Riders*, was released in 1953.

Despite a beautiful, booming voice, Eddie Dean never achieved the success on record that usually immortalizes country musicians, although he wrote two genuine classics: "One Has My Name, the Other Has My Heart" and "Hillbilly Heaven." A popular singing cowboy on film in the late 1940s, he is shown here, backed by Andy Parker and the Plainsmen, in his PRC film *Black Hills*.

Jimmy Wakely, who scored big on the record charts in the late 1940s with "One Has My Name, the Other Has My Heart" and "Slippin' Around." Popular on screen through the middle and late forties, Wakely originally started out as leader of Gene Autry's backup singers. His duets with big-band vocalist Margaret Whiting are masterpieces and started a rash of such pairings, which included George Morgan and Dinah Shore, Tennessee Ernie Ford and Kay Starr, and unlikeliest of all, Ernest Tubb and the Andrew Sisters. Wakely is still active in the West Coast club circuit. (*Jimmy Wakely*)

Roy Rogers, who stepped from singer with the Sons of the Pioneers to starring roles at Republic during the studio's salary dispute with Gene Autry. His winning personality on screen has made him a movie and television fixture, although he was never tremendously successful on record. He is shown here with his Cactus Cowboys at a wartime rodeo in Madison Square Garden. *Left to right*: Joe Caliente, Jake Watts, Rogers, Windy Bill McKay, and Bobby Gregory. (*Country Music Foundation Library and Media Center*)

Roy Rogers, Patsy Montana, Governor Green of Illinois, and Rex Allen in the late 1940s. Allen, the last of the singing cowboys, was, like Gene Autry, recruited for films from the WLS National Barn Dance in Chicago. Both his looks and his voice made him a natural for singing cowboy roles, but he appeared on the scene just as the fad was dying out. He is still frequently heard on commercials and doing narrations for Walt Disney films and television shows.

Johnny Bond came to California with Jimmy Wakely and Dick Reinhart in 1939 and soon joined Gene Autry's touring and radio show, an association that, for Bond, lasted nearly thirty years. It is his acoustic guitar playing those familiar runs on most of Gene Autry's records from that point on. Known best as a songwriter ("Cimarron," "I Wonder Where You Are Tonight"), he recorded for Columbia for years, and his two biggest records were a drinking recitation called "Ten Little Bottles" and a rockabilly tune called "Hot Rod Lincoln." This 1955 photo shows a young Freddie Hart, of "Easy Lovin' " fame, chording in the background. (*Country Music Foundation Library and Media Center*)

The ubiquitous Red River Dave in a scene from *Mexicali Rose*. A prolific songwriter and long a part of the New York country music scene, his recording of current events in song carries on the tradition of the British broadside ballad. With him are Jake Watts, Bobby Gregory, Bill Benner, and Joe Caliente. (*Country Music Foundation Library and Media Center*)

By the middle Eisenhower years, postwar realism and cynicism had written off the singing cowboy, his heroism, flashy outfits, and pauses for song in the midst of troubled times, as ill suited to a nation and a people who so recently had lived through both the horrors of real war and the wrenching adjustments to be made in coping with the hard facts of postwar life. Still, in his time the singing cowboy contributed significantly to the acceptance and growth of country music, despite his present-day status as something of an outcast.

Yet another strain had been developing in cowboy music throughout the same period, nearly as important as the cowboy star tradition but less related to film. The year was 1934, the beginning of the era of commercially oriented country music, when an authentic westerner named Tim Spencer, a Canadian singer and songwriter named Bob Nolan, and an Ohioan with a beautiful yodeling style named Len Slye teamed up to form the Pioneer Trio, a name they changed to the Sons of the Pioneers when Hugh and Karl Farr joined the group, in deference to the Farrs' largely American Indian (thus true pioneer) ancestry. Although they appeared as ranch hands and singing cowpunchers in scores of movies, they found their greatest success in the recording of songs, often from the pen of Bob Nolan, that became

An early shot of the Sons of the Pioneers, certainly the most influential and definitive western singing group. *Left to right*: Len Slye (who was to become Roy Rogers), Hugh Farr, Tim Spencer, Bob Nolan, and Karl Farr. (*Gene Bear*)

VINCE JOE DAVE HERMAN FRANK BOB

NORMAN STEWART HAMBLEN SUG

STEWART HAMBLEN AND HIS GANG—COMPLIMENTS OF The Star Outfitting Co.

Stuart Hamblen (why his name is misspelled on his own publicity photo is anybody's guess) was a popular and influential West Coast musical figure, a rough, tough Texan who was converted at a Billy Graham crusade and went on to write a host of religious and semireligious classics like "This Ole House" and "It Is No Secret What God Can Do." He even ran for President on the Prohibition ticket in 1952. He currently hosts the Cowboy Church of the Air in Los Angeles. (*Bob Pinson*)

Despite their cowboy garb, the Prairie Ramblers were one of the finest and most influential—as well as underrated—old-time string bands and were staples of the National Barn Dance for years, although their style grew increasingly toward western swing with the passing of time. Patsy Montana, with whom they toured and recorded, was the first woman singer to sell a million records—"I Want to Be a Cowboy's Sweetheart." (*Bob Pinson*)

Though not exactly a singing cowboy, Jimmie Davis (*center*) was a popular singer of country songs, most notably "You Are My Sunshine," "Nobody's Darlin'," "It Makes No Difference Now," and "Sweethearts or Strangers." Twice elected Governor of Louisiana, the handsome and charismatic Davis was a natural for movie roles. (*Bob Pinson*)

instant classics: "Way Out There," "Cool Water," and "Tumbling Tumbleweeds" were most prominent among them. Although they generated a host of imitators like Foy Willing and the Riders of the Purple Sage, the Sons of the Pioneers seemed to be the only group or indeed the only act that could sell western songs on record with any consistency (and they are still actively touring today).

For, surprising as it may seem, western music just didn't seem to sell on record, despite its popularity on screen. Jimmy Wakely's two big hits ("One Has My Name, the Other Has My Heart" and the million-selling "Slippin' Around") were pure country love songs rather than cowboy tunes. Autry, who outsold them all, had scores of hits: "Be Honest with Me," "At Mail Call Today," "Have I Told You Lately That I Love You?" "Tweedle-O-Twill," and of course "Rudolph the Red-Nosed Reindeer" (which alone accounted for nine million of the over twenty-five million sales credited to Autry). A few of Autry's big hits ("South of the Border," "Back in the Saddle Again," and "Tumbling Tumbleweeds"), however, were western songs.

Johnny Bond has a couple of amusing stories he likes to tell that demonstrate the salability of cowboy songs to country audiences, outside the realm of the silver screen: When Bond and Jimmy Wakely and Dick Reinhart were starting out in Oklahoma, they went to Dallas to try out for Columbia records, having polished their harmony singing to a Sons-of-the-Pioneers edge and having worked up some beautiful western songs, including Bond's haunting "Cimarron." They were, for all their hard work, told, "You boys sing fine; learn some honky-tonk numbers and come back and try it again." A good many years later, Bond, then a Columbia recording artist in his own right, had a battle with his A&R man over whether or not he could record "Cimarron," for he'd not only just paid $100 for a fancy arrangement but felt that his song, a classic even then (1945), was hit material—a view not shared by his A&R man, who was sure that "Cimarron," a western song, wouldn't sell. Bond finally prevailed ("Consider it a souvenir for your family," he was told): A beautiful version of "Cimarron" was cut—and, of course, sold dismally. What the public loved on the screen and in the theater they wouldn't spend cash on to buy at their local record store.

Record sales aside—as they should be, for record sales alone should never be taken as indications of either artistic merit or historic value—the influence of the singing cowboy has been tremendous. One obvious example of this influence is the use of western dress by country performers, a trend that went so far toward dying out that it's coming back as campy nostalgia in the costuming of David Allen Coe and other self-styled "rhinestone cowboys." Second, much of the national interest in the guitar can be traced to the romantic image of the singing cowboys: Although Sears Roebuck offered guitars in their ubiquitous catalog as early as 1890, guitar sales didn't become big business for them until they began marketing their Gene Autry Roundup and Melody Ranch guitars in the mid-1930s, for Autry was the first guitarist (other than, possibly, crooner Nick Lucas) to make a truly national impact with the instrument.

Yet the impact of the singing cowboy goes far beyond merely influencing costumes and popularizing guitars, although these are perhaps the most visible and therefore most obvious effects on country music. For one thing, celluloid singing cowboys brought country songs to an entire nation for the first time, for no matter how many violins eventually made their way into the arrangements (and such intrusions were not as frequent as one might think), these were basically pure country songs, concerned with the land, the life on the range, or with love. Straightforward and unaffected, they were simple, direct expressions of heartfelt feelings and made no pretense at being anything other than country songs and offered no apology for their heritage.

More to the point, there is a scene in Autry's first feature film, *Tumbling Tumbleweeds* (1935), in which Gene is beset by a couple of rough-looking hecklers while earnestly singing "That Silver Haired Daddy of Mine." Laying down his guitar, he proceeds to deal with their rudeness with his fists, and in doing so is dealing symbolically with more than poor manners: He is fighting for the dignity of the country

Handsome Bob Atcher was a staple of the Chicago country music scene for years and was one of Columbia's big sellers in the early 1940s, recording a wide variety of material that ranged from genuine folk to commercial country to cowboy. For the past sixteen years he has been mayor of the Chicago suburb of Schaumburg.

A cowboy in name only, Cowboy Copas was one of the Opry's most beloved figures. His death in 1963 cut short the comeback he was making with "Alabam." Harmonizing with him here is his daughter Kathy, with whom he frequently performed in later years.

Zeke Clements, the "Alabama Cowboy," was the Opry's first singing cowboy and was featured at times on the two other major barn dances, the National Barn Dance and the Louisiana Hayride. A prolific songwriter ("Smoke on the Water" and "Blue Mexico Skies" his biggest), he provided the voice of Bashful in Walt Disney's Snow White and the Seven Dwarfs. He is still active musically, playing tenor banjo in the Miami, Florida, area.

The Willis Brothers (*left to right*: Skeeter, Guy, and Vic) toured with Eddy Arnold as the Oklahoma Wranglers for years. Although much of their commercial success on record has come with gimmicky novelty tunes, they are actually a fine cowboy trio in the Sons of the Pioneers tradition, the last vestige of cowboy music on the Grand Ole Opry. (*Grease Brothers*)

song and the country singer. After all, the inherent worth of a country song was assumed by Autry and the singing cowboys who followed him, and their commitment was taught in turn to a generation or more of youngsters who learned by example from these films. Far from ridiculing or stripping dignity from rural music, singing cowboys in fact surrounded it with the powerful romanticism already attached to the cowboy, giving the music a good deal of the luster and the fondness America has felt for the pioneer West through the years.

Beyond legitimatizing material, the financial success enjoyed by the singing cowboys, especially Autry, helped make "hillbilly" music a respectable way of life to the musically talented and their families, thus fostering the careers of many entertainers who have followed the singing-cowboy era.

The most obvious barometer reflecting this change of attitude is the *Billboard* charts, where the term "hillbilly" was eventually (and mercifully) dropped as a means of categorizing the music and replaced with the more dignified "folk," then "country and western," attaching the attendant integrity and glamor of the movie cowboy and of the romantic West to the basically rural, southeastern country songs that always dominated the charts. It was again a significant barometer reading when the "and western" was dropped, for it meant that at last country music was ready to stand tall and on its own, embracing all its many subgenres, including even western song.

Though we may prefer to think of the singing cowboy as a rather implausible figure from our mutual pasts (it is human nature that it is difficult to take things so integrally entwined with our childhood seriously), we should spend a bit of time rethinking his importance, for the role the singing cowboy played in bringing country music to a national audience in a manner that gave it worth and dignity cannot be overestimated. Not only did he save the stagecoach from sure disaster, the cattle from stampeding, the mob from lynching an innocent man but he also propped up, fostered, and gave to country music dignity, sympathy, and credence at a time when these were sorely needed. Let us tip our hats to those men with their flashy suits, fancy guitars, and noble stallions. Without them country music might still be in a cultural backwater today, if, indeed, there existed sufficient interest in it to sustain the music at all.

Thanks, pardners.

6
CAJUN
"Big Mamou"

Cajun: often used and little understood, the word evokes images of murky Louisiana swamps, steamy bayou nights, Doug Kershaw wildly gyrating in a crushed-velvet suit, thick pots of gumbo, Longfellow's *Evangeline*, and swamp fishermen with dark, piercing eyes. It is redolent of the odor of strange food, strange speech, strange customs, and strange, urgent music, all existing far outside the mainstream of American country music, yet profoundly affecting it nonetheless.

The story of the Cajuns is a heartrending one, as befits country music legends, but it also tells much about the music and its origins. Originally settled by the French in 1604, Acadia (renamed Nova Scotia—New Scotland—by the British) was quickly though rather thinly populated by hardworking French farming people. However, the ownership of this land was under dispute for over a century—as was true of much of Canada—with both the French and British claiming it, The matter came to a head during the last four wars known to us as the French and Indian Wars, the outcome being that the island was seized by the British in a surprise attack in September 1755, and roughly ten thousand Acadians, rigidly segregated by sex—which in effect instantly divided all families—were slapped into custody and forced aboard twenty-four ships, their destination and future totally unknown to them. At home, the British took control of Acadian property, using the just-gathered harvest to feed their Continental armies.

The Acadians—those who didn't die of disease or shipwreck—were dumped from the ships rather indiscriminately at ports up and down the Atlantic coast, from Massachusetts to Georgia, even as far south as the West Indies. Their Catholic religion, their inability to speak English, and their penniless state made them outcasts wherever they disembarked. It was thus natural that the French frontier territory of Louisiana beckoned to them, despite the difficulties in getting there, if for no other reason than that its people spoke the same language and worshiped at the same church. By 1756 a small Acadian colony was formed in the territory, and

109

during the next decade thousands of homeless and homesick exiled Acadians found their way to this outpost of ex-neighbors and kin, turning the southwest part of what is now the state of Louisiana into a replica—albeit a warmer, swampier, and more fertile model—of the Acadia they had left behind.

One of the many ways in which the Acadians both consciously and unconsciously preserved their culture was in song, for they brought with them a wealth of French folk song that was, over the course of centuries, affected by many of the same cultural influences that were to infuse Anglo-Celtic folk music: black blues, Appalachian fiddle, and, later, New Orleans jazz and south-of-the-border strains. And, like rural people all over the world, they gathered at neighboring homes every so often for dances and parties, where a local fiddler and accordionist were quick to entertain the high-steppers. They sang their children to sleep with lullabies as these dances ran late into the night, and thus the phrase *fais do do*, which means in dialect to go to sleep, also came to denote home dances of this type, and even song or singing in general.

How Cajun music—the term, of course, simply an English corruption of the word *Acadian*—came to employ the fiddle is fairly obvious, for it was a folk instrument popular over most of Europe and the New World even at the time of colonization. Their wholehearted acceptance of the accordion is a bit more puzzling: The type of accordion played by Cajun musicians today was first invented in Vienna in 1829, and it is thought that the instrument was adopted from German immigrants passing westward through Louisiana. In fact, German culture seems to have influenced the music more than once, and it may be that the passion for waltzes and the heavy, insistent beat so frequently found in Cajun music were both grafted onto French and French-American folk music during the days of cultural interchange with Teutonic immigrants.

Harry Choates at the mike, a rare photo of a man rarely photographed. Although the band he's with looks western swing in instrumentation, Choates' sound was strictly deep Cajun. (*Bob Pinson*)

Certainly as much was gained from musical blacks and Creoles, who adapted the blues from their African and slave culture toward the French-speaking culture in which they thrived in Louisiana. In fact, a great many early recordings of Cajun music were by black or Creole singers and musicians, most prominent among them Àmedee Ardoin, who recorded for Brunswick in the days of acoustical recording (although credit for the first Cajun recording generally goes to white accordionist Joseph Falcon, whose "Allons à LaFayette" was cut in 1928).

At any rate, with the coming of age of the phonograph record, a market small in geographical area but large in population and willingness to buy records of this peculiar music was discovered by the major record companies, and while these recorded efforts are often crude (though surely not more crude than comparable recordings of mountain string bands), they were also powerful and evocative, mainly to a region, but increasingly to a nation as well.

With the passing of years, Cajun music was to both add to and absorb musical strains from the increasingly popular country music of the era, with which it coexisted nearly side by side. As playing for dances continued to be by far the major outlet of musical talents, Cajun music began to draw heavily from the feeling of western swing and from New Orleans jazz, although the music never for a moment lost its distinctive feel—its very bilingualism assured that.

Despite roots in east Texas and Louisiana, Moon Mullican was no Cajun. However, his recording of Harry Choates' "Jole Blon" was the one most popular in country music.

Although Rusty and Doug were the Opry's first concession to rockabilly music in the late 1950s, Doug Kershaw emerged a decade later to bring his exuberant style and Cajun music to a national audience with "Louisiana Man," his autobiographical tribute to growing up Cajun.

Jimmy Newman, from Big Mamou, Louisiana, was the first big-time popularizer of the Cajun sound on the Grand Ole Opry. His greatest successes came with popular country material, but he never let his audiences forget his Cajun heritage.

The 1930s brought continued commercial success, especially in the recording field, for groups like the Hackberry Ramblers, but it was the 1940s that proved to be the pivotal decade for the music, for it was then that its largest national audience was achieved, mainly through the songwriting ability of Harry Choates, a Hank Williams-like young fiddler and singer who died in jail at twenty-eight, burned out by the raw, tempestuous life he'd lived. Although apparently not a Cajun by descent, Choates grew up in thoroughly Cajun culture, yet was able to play with country bands of the place and time. Choates developed a large and widely enthusiastic following with compositions like "Poor Hobo," "Catting Around," and "Port Arthur Waltz." His song "Jole Blon"—which means simply "pretty blond," in French dialect—was a tremendous seller, however, for Moon Mullican and Roy Acuff as well as Choates himself, and it was this song, now a standard, that thrust a degree of national prominence upon him. But he was a rough, raw young man, and his taste for alcohol and the honky-tonk life kept him poor and limited much of his career to work as a sideman in taverns or to playing fiddle in country bands. He had been living in Austin, Texas, for roughly three years when he was jailed for wife and child desertion. Apparently he had already developed cirrhosis of the liver while in his mid-twenties, and the shock of sobering up in the jail cell proved too much for his frail system. Within three days of his arrest he was dead, far from the warm bayous of his native Louisiana. An elusive figure, Choates' life is still shrouded in mystery, and even photographs of this first Cajun national star are rare.

Hank Williams himself had a tremendous popularizing effect on Cajun music with his classic "Jambalaya." Having appeared over KWKH's Louisiana Hayride in Shreveport both before he joined the Opry and after he left it, Williams was particularly fond of the area and of the Cajun lifestyle and joyfully shouted the pleasures of Acadian living on record and in person with this song. Catching the gaiety and infectiousness of Cajun music on a strictly country record, Williams was able to sing a moving paean to at least one aspect—the carefree, happy side—of the life and music of the bayou fisherman, descendant of the uprooted Acadian of nearly two centuries before him.

Another popularizer of the music on a wider level is Jimmy Newman, a young Cajun singer who achieved national success with his high, crooning singing, both on record ("A Fallen Star" and "Cry, Cry Darlin'" were his big hits) and on the Grand Ole Opry since 1956. But although standard country love songs are his forte, he is unashamed of his Cajun heritage, proudly proclaiming his birthplace, Big Mamou, and features frequent Cajun songs, both in French and in English, on his live shows, Opry appearances, and to a lesser extent on record, although he did record a fine album called "Folk Songs from the Bayou Country." It was Newman who brought the high, piercing, exuberant, joyful cry of the Cajun musician—"aai-eeeee"—to the Opry stage and to national prominence. And it is an interesting and revealing sidelight that Newman's longtime fiddler Rufus Thibodeaux (there's a Cajun name for you!), who is equally at home on Newman's straight country songs as well as on the Cajun numbers, also toured with Bob Wills and his Texas Playboys—an example of the frequent and fertile musical cross-pollenization that occurred between western Louisiana and eastern Texas.

During the late 1950s a hitch in the service broke up an exciting rockabilly duet that had come to the Opry only shortly before the draft called. Known as Rusty and Doug, they brought to the Opry stage high-spirited Cajun music strongly influenced by country stylings as well as the pulse of rock and roll, which was having its effect on them as it was on most of their young contemporaries. The duet team of Rusty and Doug didn't survive the slack period of country music that followed their return from military service, but Doug Kershaw kept struggling along, writing and performing, before finally breaking loose in the late 1960s with his intense, sharply etched autobiographical portrait of growing up a poor Cajun, "Louisiana Man." It may be that Kershaw's flamboyant dress, striking looks, gyrating stage manner, intense and electric presence on camera and in person are more important elements of his popularity than his use of Cajun themes and material. There is little doubt, however, that he is the real thing, and despite his crushed-velvet suits and his way of holding the fiddle against his chest, Doug Kershaw is bringing to a wide cross-section of American youth—for his popularity is with the young, rock-oriented audience, not the traditional country fan—a glimpse of a rich culture, which, despite its small size and heartrending history, has affected, in its way, the course of several segments of country music, of American music in general, and of American life.

Then, too, as interest in American folk song, folklore, folk arts, and folk life has grown in the past two decades, not infrequently the spotlight has been turned upon Cajun music and musicians, and national folk festivals, attended by thousands, generally feature at least one representative of traditional Cajun music, usually to the delight of an audience that has had little or no contact with this pulsating, emotional musical form.

A couple of recent records that climbed high on the country charts (though to call them true hits would stretch the point a bit) prove that the country/Cajun musical interchange continues: "Big Mamou" and "Colinda," traditional Cajun songs performed by a group little known nationally called Fiddlin' Frenchie Burke and the Outlaws, were not only sung bilingually but featured Cajun calls and fiddle style laid over the solid bedrock of pure honky-tonk country instrumentals and vocal delivery. Nice records, both of them, and captivating for their vital, exciting mixture of musical styles.

At its heart Cajun music is very like old-time country music: emotional, stimulating, filled with an inner tension. Alternately sad and gay, it is the remnant of the folk music of a rural agrarian people that speaks strongly to them and, empathetically, to us. Despite the barriers that culture and language impose, it has given much to the development of country music, for it reveals without affectation the experience and emotions common to all mankind.

7
BLUEGRASS
"Blue Moon of Kentucky"

Bluegrass music stands today in a swirling whirlpool of paradox: While thousands gladly brave stone-age conditions and blistering heat or pouring rain to attend festivals in such unlikely and out-of-the-way spots as Bean Blossom, Indiana, and Watermelon Park, near Berryville, Virginia, major record labels despair at their inability to sell bluegrass records. While the main attraction to musician and fan alike has been the music's stubborn and hearteningly successful determination to prove its worth as a traditional music form in the face of rapid change and the pressures of commercialism, there is simultaneous pressure from a very large segment of fans and musicians who seek to create, to change, to modernize, to expand frontiers. Finally, while it is a music lovingly and hauntingly described as having a "high, lonesome sound," it is in fact most frequently performed with an aggressive, athletic feel, the beauty of the music and the emotion of the singing buried under show-off musicianship, having all the subtlety and sensitivity of a hundred-yard dash. These and a dozen other paradoxes abound in this music, reflecting the turmoil often associated with rapid, unstructured growth—a dozen different people will offer a dozen different opinions as to the roots, important figures, and future of the music, as well as to the methods needed to continue its growth and success.

Its recent success has indeed been remarkable: I remember clearly the magic, mystical feeling surrounding Carlton Haney's second bluegrass festival only a decade ago. The few hundred of us there were awed and inspired (Haney still maintains it was the "best festival ever"), yet the electric excitement was tinged with a pervading touch of sadness: We felt we were watching the dying gasp of a beautiful, intricate, delicate art form, soon to be lost with other atavistic but precious treasures of the past. We felt we were participating in a loving last look at an important and sadly neglected segment of musical history as we watched Clyde Moody, Mac Wiseman, and Jimmy Martin being reunited with Bill Monroe after all those years, and felt transported, in very nearly a religious sense, to new realms of

In the dressing room at the Grand Ole Opry. (*Grease Brothers*)

Cashing in on the "Bonnie and Clyde" syndrome in the late 1960s was carried to its logical ultimate by an Oregon-based group called the Sawtooth Mountain Volunteers. (*Steve Waller*)

musical understanding as the Osborne Brothers and Monroe sang the ethereal trio "I Hear a Sweet Voice Calling." It seemed a fitting epitaph to this achingly beautiful yet electrically exciting music, ruefully outdated by time and custom.

Today, ten years later, scores of bluegrass festivals crowd the summer months, attended by hundreds of thousands of fans and supporting at least a dozen new professional bands. How wrong we were as we mourned on those rolling hills of Cantrell's Horse Farm, near Fincastle, Virginia, that sunny Labor Day weekend in 1966: We weren't presiding over last rites, we were watching the beginnings of the rebirth of a musical form so dramatic that the impact generated there has not yet been fully felt and certainly not fully understood by the music's fans or by the musicians themselves. Today this impact continues to send ripples and shock waves through the country music community, causing wrenching paradox to proceed hand in hand with explosive growth.

The roots of bluegrass go all the way back, as Bill Monroe is fond of saying, to the Scottish bagpipes of his ancestors on one hand, and on the other to the Negro blues, which Monroe learned from a guitarist and fiddler named Arnold Shultz in the small western Kentucky town of Rosine. Here Bill, the youngest of eight children, was first exposed to music, both from his fiddling and accordion-playing mother and from his older brothers as well, particularly Birch and Charlie, who were to carve careers as professional musicians in years to come. By the time Bill reached the age of eleven, however, both his parents had died and his older brothers had moved off to the industrial North to work. He then entered an extremely difficult though significant period in his life, spending several years living with his uncle Pen, his mother's brother, who was a local swapper of anything that came to hand by profession and a fiddler by avocation. Here young Bill absorbed his uncle's zest for music, often accompanying the old man on guitar at local dances, and it was also at this time that he fell under the influence of Shultz, who, with his bluesy singing and guitar playing and fine old-fashioned fiddling, was a unique and unforgettable teacher.

The earliest known picture, taken in the late 1920s, of Charlie and Bill Monroe playing music together. They had not yet embarked on a career as professional musicians. (*Charlie Monroe*)

117

Bill Monroe ca. 1942, with a pre-banjo version of his Bluegrass Boys. *Left to right*: Art Wooten, Monroe, "Cousin Wilbur" Westbrook, and Pete Pyle, later to lead his own band on the Opry.

Bill eventually joined his brothers Birch and Charlie in Whiting, Indiana, and after a period marked by intense practice, hard work at a Sinclair Oil refinery, and as part of a team of square dancers on the WLS National Barn Dance (where the brothers were influenced musically by groups like Mac and Bob, Karl and Harty, and the Prairie Ramblers), Bill and Charlie decided to try to make a go of it as one of the guitar–mandolin duets becoming popular in the early 1930s. They soon became the most popular of them all. Although the brothers were frequently in personal disagreement, they complemented each other well on stage and on record: Bill, always painfully shy because of his crossed eyes (since corrected) and his position as the "baby" of the family, turned his pain and passion inward to his music, developing a fiery, exciting style on the mandolin that far surpassed the efforts of his contemporaries, and sang in a high, blues-edged tenor voice. Charlie, who was tall, athletic, handsome, and outgoing, was a fine rhythm guitar player with a strong, insistent style and a clean, clear lead voice. Unlike the introspective Bill, Charlie put much of his effort into his stage work, his audience contact. Together they became the most exciting, most commanding duet of the 1930s. But eventually personality conflicts became too strong, and in 1938 they split up. Charlie went on to form a group he called his Kentucky Pardners, who were among country music's more popular recording and road bands for the next decade and a half. And Bill formed his Blue Grass Boys, whose sound and style and even name would revolutionize an entire segment of country music—a revolution that continues today.

Just when bluegrass as a musical entity came into being has been a matter of debate, sometimes heated debate. Some say it was about 1940, when Bill combined the hard-driving old-time guitar style (best exemplified by his brother Charlie) with a bluesy timing (perhaps the influence of Shultz), which gave a particular swing and bounce to what was basically in form an old-time string band, a feel that makes Monroe's first recordings for RCA as a solo singer and bandleader so dramatic and different. (Incidentally, it is Monroe himself playing guitar on his classic reworking of Jimmie Rodgers' "Muleskinner Blues": He claimed no other guitarist could play the rhythm he felt and heard within him.) Others argue that there was no such thing as bluegrass until 1945, when nineteen-year-old Earl Scruggs joined the Blue Grass Boys, bringing with him that insistent, rhythmic, syncopated, driving three-finger banjo style Opry mentor George D. Hay used to call "his fancy banjo." And still others maintain that bluegrass was not a style—it was just Bill Monroe's music, much as Ernest Tubb had his music, his sound—until 1948, when the sound was deliberately copied by a couple of Virginia youngsters called the Stanley Brothers.

At any rate, Monroe's sound was personal—though not unique—when he joined the Opry in 1939. If there existed any really distinctive sound that set him apart from the other Opry string bands in the late 1930s, it was not the subtle rhythm he imparted to the band sound or even his dramatic and exciting mandolin playing: It was his high, piercing, rafter-reaching voice, intense and sincere, crackling off crisp yodels that made you sit up and shake your head in amazement—a fact all too easily forgotten today as bluegrass has come to be dominated by red-hot instrumentalists with rather mechanical approaches to singing.

Earl Scruggs, the man who brought the banjo from its role as a comedian's musical rouser to an instantly identifiable and distinctive musical sound. Rarely has one man so revolutionized the sound and style of a single musical instrument.

Yet the reason for a fascination with and focus upon instrumentals in contemporary bluegrass music is easy to understand, for the whole world of country music seemed to turn its head in excited surprise in 1945, when Earl Scruggs, a shy, quiet kid from near Shelby, North Carolina, joined Bill's Blue Grass Boys. Having perfected an intricate, complex three-finger roll (inherited from gifted but less creative forbears like Snuffy Jenkins), Scruggs simply revolutionized the use of the five-string banjo in American music, and all those ads you hear today, with a sparkling banjo rippling behind words of praise for Dole pineapples, Mazda and Datsun automobiles, and a score of other products, are testaments to the revolution wrought by this kid and his "fancy banjo."

The band Scruggs joined—mellow-voiced Lester Flatt on guitar, bluesy Floridian Chubby Wise on fiddle, and solid Cedric Rainwater on bass—is considered by many to be the finest version of the Blue Grass Boys ever to have existed. They played fast, they played clean, they sang impeccable harmony, and Monroe and Flatt found in each other sympathetic talents for songwriting, and thus many—perhaps most—of the songs considered to be classics in the form were written by one or the other or both in the heyday of the band, from 1945–1948. Monroe's bands have included brilliant musicians ever since, but that particular group was a very special one, full of excitement and confidence and the exhilaration of creation. Since they were together for nearly three years (rare with Monroe, as with many hard-traveling bands), they developed a smooth cohesiveness and a highly polished sound that have set them still further apart from later versions of the Blue Grass Boys.

The Stanley Brothers (Ralph *at left* and Carter *at right*) as they looked when starting out at the famous bluegrass station WCYB in Bristol. Their fringed jackets, no matter how attractive, were incongruous with their mournful mountain sound.

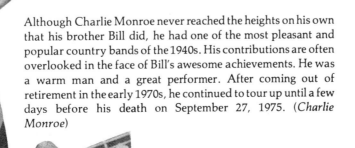

Although Charlie Monroe never reached the heights on his own that his brother Bill did, he had one of the most pleasant and popular country bands of the 1940s. His contributions are often overlooked in the face of Bill's awesome achievements. He was a warm man and a great performer. After coming out of retirement in the early 1970s, he continued to tour up until a few days before his death on September 27, 1975. (*Charlie Monroe*)

121

Don Reno and Red Smiley and the Tennessee Cutups were one of the earliest bluegrass groups to begin experimenting with the traditional bluegrass sound, accented by Reno's brilliant, jazzy, and inventive banjo style. With them are Mac Magaha on fiddle and John Palmer on bass.

In 1948, however, this magic grouping of musicians and singers split up. Both Flatt and Scruggs, weary of endless touring, retired from the music business to take up day jobs, a course of action that didn't last long. By late in the same year they had teamed up with each other to form a new bluegrass band, which they called the Foggy Mountain Boys, a group that was to become by far the most widely known and successful bluegrass band of all.

Musicians came and went from Monroe's band in the late 1940s and early 1950s, and if his music wasn't as polished as when Flatt and Scruggs were Blue Grass Boys, it became even more intense and personal. It was really in this period that the "high, lonesome sound" developed, for Monroe, continually changing and intensifying his music, delved into mournful harmony singing, radically changed his mandolin playing from the fast, fluid style he'd made famous to an abrupt, emotion-filled attack, and began writing highly personal songs of lost love and of death.

The musicians who played for a time with the Blue Grass Boys during this period amount to a collection of bluegrass all-stars, for many were to achieve great success on their own much later, in and out of the field of bluegrass, and most are still active and popular today. They include Mac Wiseman, Jimmy Martin, Vassar Clements, Don Reno, Jim Smoak, Carter Stanley, Benny Martin, Gordon Terry, Jim Eanes, and Sonny Osborne.

All fads—even good ones, even good musical ones—must come to an end at some time, however, and by the late 1950s the public demand for bluegrass had ebbed. It had been accepted as a valid musical style and was enjoyed by a fair number of

Lester Flatt and Earl Scruggs not long after they joined the Opry in the mid 1950s. *Left to right*: Paul Warren (still with Flatt), Scruggs, Curly Seckler, and Flatt. (*Country Music Foundation Library and Media Center*)

people, but there no longer existed the kind of excitement generated by the Monroe–Flatt–Scruggs version of the Blue Grass Boys a decade earlier. In fact, Monroe frequently had trouble keeping a band together at all in those dark days, and precious few other bluegrass bands were making any kind of a living at the music. Flatt and Scruggs were the only exception, for they had found a genial and generous sponsor in Martha White Mills, and they augmented their touring and recording income with both television and radio programs for the Martha White Flour Company. In addition to a natural decline, the sudden explosion of rock, which drained young listeners away from all specialized fields of music, hurt traditional country music (with which bluegrass was firmly associated by this time) more than any other. Hundreds of "hard" country acts died on the vine during those troubled times, and this included many bluegrass bands; it almost looked as though the music was heading for an inevitable and unhappy end.

What saved it was, oddly enough, a feeling not unlike that which made the rise of rock possible: disaffection on the part of American youth of all regions from the dreamy, romantic, but somehow enervated, superficial, and stylized popular music of the early and middle 1950s. A young radio audience rejected what music programmers call "easy listening" today: the music of Frank Sinatra, Jo Stafford, and Tony Bennett. This disaffection from a complacent and hypocritical American society led some to seek and find truth in the raw sensuality of rock, while others turned to the native folk musics of this and other societies in an attempt to return to some basic truths and traditions forgotten by our rootless and plasticized society. It was this disaffected group that, in the late 1950s, found an active and vital inheritor of the Anglo-Celtic folk tradition in bluegrass (especially in that it preserved so much of an older folk repertoire). By the early 1960s bluegrass had made a small comeback and was being heard in college concert halls, at the Newport Folk Festivals, on television's "Hootenanny" show, and even in Carnegie Hall. The sound of bluegrass had reached a sufficient level of national recognition to allow its use in the theme music for the long-running television series "The Beverly Hillbillies," and Flatt and Scruggs' recording of the theme was the first (and, until the theme from the film *Deliverance*, the only) bluegrass recording ever to reach number one on the charts.

But however much prestige was gained from such appearances, concerts, and television exposure, most bluegrass entertainers were still forced to earn the bulk of their living much as they had done fifteen years earlier: small shows in schoolhouses and theaters, with even these becoming ever less lucrative as time went on. So the degree of national prominence bluegrass was able to achieve during that period did not actually have much immediate effect on the professional musicians and the music—it was to come later, much more subtly. This is why the second bluegrass festival, in 1966, was such a moving event for those who attended it: Although the crowd was bigger than at the first festival the year before, it still numbered only a few hundred, and promoter Carlton Haney lost a good bit of money on the event (as he had on the first festival); the show represented a labor of love on his part. While many looked forward to next year's festival with enthusiasm, there was an all-

Brash, aggressive Jimmy Martin brings a lot of his personality into his exciting and banjo-oriented version of the bluegrass sound. After spending years with Bill Monroe, he went off to form one of the most consistent bands—in both sound and popularity—in the field. One of the engagements of which he is most proud is a stint at the Golden Nugget in the early 1960s; with him are (*left to right*) Kirk Hansard, Paul Williams, Lois Johnson, Bill Emerson, and Zeb Collins. (*Country Music Foundation Library and Media Center*)

Hylo Brown, an alumnus of the Flatt and Scruggs band, led his own excellent band, the Timberliners, for several years, sponsored, like the Foggy Mountain Boys, by Martha White Flour. Although he has drifted into relative obscurity in recent years, his first album on Capitol, titled simply "Hylo Brown," is a treasured collector's item, for it is some of the best bluegrass music ever recorded. With him in this 1959 photo is probably his best band: (*left to right*) "Tater" Tate, Red Rector, Brown, Jim Smoak, and "Flapjack" on the bass. Kneeling is another comedian, "Little Darlin'." (*Jim Smoak*)

pervading sadness clouding the excitement, for this might well be the last gasp of both the festivals and, indeed, of the music itself.

But the following year's festival was a surprise. An appreciably larger crowd turned up at the new site, an old country show park on a riverbank called Watermelon Park, near Berryville, Virginia. What's more, in June Bill Monroe set up a festival of his own (which he called, with characteristic Scottish stubborn desire to go against the grain, a "bluegrass celebration") in Bean Blossom, Indiana, at a small, ill-equipped country music park he had owned—although it was managed by aging brother Birch—for years. The following year crowds at both festivals were still larger.

The trend continued to accelerate, and by the late 1960s a few things were becoming clear; most importantly that bluegrass, through the vehicle of the festival, had found a whole new outlet and was on the verge of being able to support as many or more professional bands than it had during its peak years of the late 1940s and early 1950s—the years when, because of the number of bands playing in Monroe's style, someone began referring to the music in general by the name of Monroe's band, "Bluegrass" (as if we now had "texasplayboys" music instead of western swing).

Other trends were appearing simultaneously. For one thing, promoters were running out of surprises. Bill Monroe reunited with Mac Wiseman or with Jimmy Martin for the first time in a decade (or with Clyde Moody for the first time in more than two!) was an unsurpassed thrill at first but wore a bit thin—for the performers as well as the audience—after repeated reunions and staged "stories of bluegrass." Besides, with the explosive growth in sheer numbers of festivals, it became no longer physically possible for the same musicians to attend all festivals anyway. Legendary singers and musicians—Charlie Monroe, Red Smiley, the Blue Sky Boys—were coaxed out of retirement. Flatt and Scruggs at last began to make long-awaited appearances (separately—they split in 1969, Flatt returning to the easygoing country-style bluegrass he was obviously comfortable with, Scruggs continuing, with the help of his sons, to experiment with the folk-rock sound that increasingly characterized the later albums of the duo). These and other expedients were tried, but the only thing that proved to save the festivals from staleness was the influence of new groups, new talent, new ideas, new songs.

Pioneered by a Washington, D.C., group called the Country Gentlemen in the late 1950s, what has come to be called progressive bluegrass or sometimes "newgrass" was a direct and deliberate alternative to the somber, serious, intense, and sometimes pompous classic bluegrass of Monroe and the Stanley Brothers. This musical hybrid offered flashy, experimental music with heavy borrowings from folk, jazz, and blues; a large dose of humor in choice of songs, between-songs comment, and often in raucous stage antics; and a generally irreverent look at the traditional strictures of both the music and even of life itself. What these progressive, newgrass groups lack in depth of feeling—the "soul" of bluegrass if you will—they make up for in contemporary material, exciting musical experiment, and appeal to a much broader audience.

A third musical direction, distinct from both classic bluegrass and newgrass, has been pursued by Lester Flatt, Jim and Jesse, and, to a greater extent, the Osborne Brothers. Not content either to please the old hard-line fan and traditionalist on one hand or to cater to the new, younger, rock-oriented convert on the other, these bands, as a group, strive to integrate much of the traditional sound of bluegrass with contemporary country sounds and stylings, a hybrid that has, to some degree, been quite successful. The Osborne Brothers, consistently good record sellers, even have

Long the pioneers in the progressive sound, here the Country Gentlemen engage in some onstage antics for a 1971 Opry crowd. The comic aspect has helped them maintain their tremendous audience appeal. Guitarist Charlie Waller has preserved the band's sound through numerous personnel changes; with him here are Bill Emerson on banjo, Doyle Lawson on mandolin, and Bill Yates on bass. (*Les Leverett*)

had a few impressive hits ("Rocky Top" was their biggest) and were voted Vocal Group of the Year in the 1971 Country Music Association Awards Show, televised nationally.

While such diversity is a sure sign of a vigorous and thriving music, it also has led to considerable controversy and division among fans and performers. The sometimes narrow world of bluegrass (some segments of which would like to cut themselves off completely from all other forms of country music) spends a great deal of time heatedly discussing electric amplificaton versus the traditional acoustic sound and arguing over the appropriateness of this or that selection or instrument or arrangement. There is no doubt that the provincial, protective atmosphere that once cloaked the music and characterized the majority of its fans is disappearing, as it must if bluegrass is to continue to grow, as those who seek to protect it claim to

Jim (*right*) and Jesse McReynolds carrying on the tradition of brother duets, they incorporated it right into the mainstream of bluegrass, and their spectacular and moving harmony singing have made them perennial favorites, despite their occasional forays into the field of modern country music. (*Grease Brothers*)

The Osborne Brothers were the first and most successful group to blend the sound of commercial country music with that of traditional bluegrass, and despite the uproar this caused in the sometimes small world of bluegrass, they have won a wide following across a broad spectrum of country music. With Bob (*left*) and Sonny Osborne is their longtime guitarist Dale Sledd.

Larry Sparks, a quiet young man who is carrying on the ultra-traditional mountain sound of the Stanley Brothers with his songwriting, singing, and his band, the Lonesome Ramblers.

Bill Monroe today. (*Carl Fleischhauer*)

desire. But at the same time bluegrass is losing something: A music most fans turned to because they found its stubborn refusal to commercialize a refreshing virtue is now, by and large, making every effort to change, to become more commercial, to appeal to more and more fans regardless of the costs, accepting the hallowed American tradition that growth and size are the ultimate and worthy goals, that bigness is better. Rather than "converting" new fans to bluegrass, bluegrass is instead converting itself to meet the needs of new fans, and with the exception of the rock-ribbed Bill Monroe and Ralph Stanley bands (and a very few younger bands in the traditional mold, such as the Lonesome Ramblers, headed by Larry Sparks), this is the direction the music is taking at an increasingly rapid rate.

Obviously there is much of value in bluegrass music. It wouldn't appeal to so many, over so broad a spectrum of social status, age, and geography, if there was not. But it is an unusual paradox that the values through which fans are drawn to the music are the very ones being discarded in the music's search for a fresher, more contemporary sound.

Yet no music—especially no music so obviously thriving as bluegrass is today—can remain a museum piece except under the most artificially controlled conditions. Bluegrass has often been compared to Dixieland jazz in its use of interpretive, freewheeling instrumental breaks within a basically rigid structure, and the comparison seems a good one, for it won't be long, I suspect, before traditional bluegrass does become a museum piece, as did New Orleans jazz, while progressive bluegrass continues to evolve, as later jazz evolved out of Dixieland. In two or three decades, after the passing of the great masters (many have gone already: Red Smiley, Carter Stanley), certain traditionalists will seek to re-create the classic sounds of various bands and eras, much as a number of Dixieland bands do today, while the progressivists will have developed the music into something entirely different, unknown and unknowable to us here and now. These traditionalist bands will be few, exaggerating a trend already strongly in evidence. Perhaps there'll even be a newgrass nostalgia band centered around the 1975 era. Who knows?

Despite the problems that plague this tradition, no aspect of currently active country music is as likely to live on in live performance as is bluegrass. At the same time, the modern sound of bluegrass will carry on its two-way integration currently underway with pop, rock, folk, and underground music, continually evolving into whatever it is that progressive bluegrass will become.

All this is ultimately to the good, for such widespread interest in the music will continuously lead a small percentage of new fans to explore the roots lying beneath the altered surface of bluegrass today, and long after the peculiar time, place, and culture that spawned this music have disappeared into the mists of time, the music called bluegrass will provide a subtle and sensitive insight into a past not retrievable by any other means.

8
WESTERN SWING
"Home in San Antone"

It must have been those empty, endless plains, those "wide open spaces," those lonely acres stretching flat and finely divided against the sky as far as the eye can see.

They say there's a spot in west Texas where you can stand and see the towns of Midland, twenty-five miles in one direction, and Odessa, twenty-five miles in another. Such breadth of vision doubtless had a powerful effect on the settlers who left the snug Appalachians and comfortable rolling hills of Tennessee and Virginia to make their new homes in the lonely prairie lands of the Southwest. While their forbears and contemporaries remained warmly surrounded by family, friends, and the life-giving hills, the pioneers who settled and raised families in the flat prairie land of Texas and Oklahoma had little contact with neighbors and kin and were surrounded by the howling prairie wind instead of the solid rock of the mountains they'd left behind.

It must have been this isolation, this loneliness, this desperate need for personal contact, for community activity, and even for pure fun that caused the particular style of music called western swing to develop and flourish in the flat Southwest.

This social need was something entirely different from the sources from which the music sprang—the Appalachian fiddle, the slight Mariachi flavor, the big-city jazz feel of the soloists, the big-band sound it strove so to imitate. This need was a very human thing, a very personal thing, and it was far different from that felt by southeasterners of the same period. In the Southeast, social needs were filled by closeness of kin and by the physical presence of the warm (although often far from rich) mountains and foothills—a presence that seemed somehow to affirm continually strong religious beliefs. It was as if the commanding, nurturing, everlasting hills were daily reminders of God and His presence. The Southwest, on the other hand, offered millions of acres of flat, sunbaked prairie, and with them hot, hard work, aching loneliness, and the intense need to break loose from the grinding, dusty toil to be with neighbors, dance with neighbors, even raise a little hell with neighbors.

Bob Wills (*left*) and Spade Cooley.

The early settlers brought with them the southeastern practice of gathering at a different neighbor's house every Saturday night for a "house party": rolling back the rugs and dancing to the tunes of the area's old-time fiddler. After the turn of the century, however, the spirit of these occasions began gradually to evolve into two different activities in the two different regions. In the Southeast, the emphasis of such gatherings came to rest upon the music and the musicians, and the dancing, while still the most important aspect of the festivities, remained centered around high-spirited but chaste square dances. Westerners, however, developed a taste for slower, slightly more physical (and "modern") two-steps. In addition, the religious overtones that seemed to pervade house parties in the Southeast appeared somewhat diminished on the prairie and the use of alcohol became, if not more prevalent than in the Southeast, at least more overt and somehow more acceptable in the wilder West.

Less encumbered by religious strictures (although not unaffected by the guilt syndrome that is so much a part of country music, regardless of era or region), the southwesterners developed a different set of musical needs: In other words, what has come to be called western swing developed more out of the needs of its listeners than out of a fusion of musical styles. Such an argument perhaps belabors the obvious: A musical style may be created by the talent or genius of one individual or one band, but to attain popularity, it must fill a specific need or set of needs for a great number of people. And the needs to socialize, to dance, to "let go," all were met by that danceable musical style called western swing.

The house parties eventually moved to barns to accommodate the crowds of farmers and merchants from far-flung areas, and fiddlers added musicians and instruments to their bands both to make the music loud enough to fill the larger spaces of the barn and to imitate in country music fashion the popular dance music of the era, for above all the throngs wanted to dance.

Eventually, in the larger cow and oil towns that were fast becoming cities, barn dances were moved to dance halls, in which a ring of tables surrounded the huge dance floor, which faced the band—a band that had continued to grow in size: first five, then nine, twelve, even up to eighteen pieces. Later electric amplification was added for both the steel and standard guitars, and microphones and public-address

Although this shot is from a movie, *Square Dance Jubilee* (1949), the scene is not atypical of square dances done before large western swing bands. (*Country Music Foundation Library and Media Center*)

Bob Wills' first band, the Playboys, in Waco, Texas, in October 1933. They changed their name to the Texas Playboys when they moved to KVOO in Tulsa. *Left to right*: June Whalen, Kermit Whalen, Bob Wills, Johnnie Lee Wills, Tommy Duncan, and announcer Everett Stover. (*Bob Pinson*)

W. Lee O'Daniel used his popularity as a songwriter, announcer, and bandleader of the Light Crust Doughboys to propel himself to first the Texas governor's chair, then the U.S. Senate. Bob Wills started with the band before forming his Texas Playboys. This early 1933 photo shows (*left to right*) O'Daniel, Wills, Herman Arnspiger, Tommy Duncan, Sleepy Johnson, and the bus driver, Henry Steinbarth, standing before their transportation.

An automobile accident cut short the promising career of Milton Brown and His Musical Brownies. Brown, formerly a vocalist with the Light Crust Doughboys, spun off from O'Daniel's organization and recorded several popular and promising sides for the Bluebird label. The Musical Brownies, shown here late in 1935 (not long before Brown's death), are (*left to right*) Wanna Coffman, Cecil Brower, Bob Dunn, Cliff Bruner, Fred "Papa" Calhoun, Milton Brown, Ocie Stockard, and Durwood Brown. (*Bob Pinson*)

systems for the fiddles and increasingly important vocalists, who were developing a deep-pitched, sun-warmed, semicrooning style, a combination of Jimmie Rodgers and Bing Crosby, as opposed to the higher-pitched, emotion-filled eastern style, typified by Roy Acuff and Molly O'Day.

The names of these dance halls, like Crystal Springs, Cain's Academy, and the Trianon Ballroom, became synonymous with the growing musical style, and a Texas or Oklahoma dance hall on a Saturday night was a special world unto itself, one that has faded and passed with the music that created it. In its glory, however, the dance hall flourished with a tangy flair unique and marvelous in American life. Typically, the stage area was surrounded by band lovers (or dancers taking breaks), admiring the "hot licks" and subtle musical interplay of the band as it worked, often nonstop—one band member at a time stepping offstage periodically for a break. Behind this ring of eager onlookers might be hundreds of hot, sweaty dancers crowding the hardwood floor, their shoes—if their sense of time was good —sounding like a giant soft snare drum as they waltzed to "Westphalia Waltz" or two-stepped to "San Antonio Rose." It is an interesting and unique holdover from the days of the house party and the barn dance that occasionally (and frequently only regionally) some arcane and complicated dance such as the schottische or the Paul Jones was undertaken by some dancers in the crowd. A throwback to an earlier era, these atavistic dance forms failed to make the transition to California, when for a while in the late 1940s and the early 1950s that state became the headquarters for many of the swing bands and the location of hundreds of dance halls, where more and more physical contact and hard drinking were the order of the day.

Encircling the floor in a typical dance hall of either the Southwest or California in this era were tables where dancers rested, flirted, watched the action on the floor or at neighboring tables, sometimes fought, and drank—openly where it was legal and covertly where it was not—to the music of Bob Wills and his Texas Playboys or any other of a hundred imitative and/or derivative bands.

With any historical movement of any kind there is always a central figure whose career—be it in politics, business, or entertainment—parallels the growth, development, and the inevitable decline of that movement. To the musical movement called western swing, Bob Wills is certainly that figure. For it was he who shaped the disparate musical elements into a style that so filled and fitted the needs of thousands of people for so long. He was not actually the first practitioner of western swing, but was easily its most towering, dominating figure.

Raised on a hardscrabble farm just outside of Turkey, Texas, Wills learned fiddling from his father and eventually gave up the plow to ply his musical craft on a medicine show, doing blackface comedy and selling medical nostrums in addition to his fiddling. Although he barbered in and around Turkey, Wills was a popular musician at house parties, barn dances, and fiddling contests. Though a fine old-time fiddler, his magnetic personality was becoming his dominant characteristic even then. In 1930 he helped form a new organization that came to be called (after their sponsor) the Light Crust Doughboys—a name spontaneously invented their first time on the air in Fort Worth—and it proved to be a band receptive to fresh and

Maybe the classic Texas Playboys band. Three fiddles and horns highlighted the danceable sound, yet the steel guitar kept the distinct country feel that characterized Wills at his peak. *Left to right*: Everett Stover (trumpet), Leon McAuliffe (steel), Charles Laughton (sax), O. W. Mayo (manager), Zeb McNally (sax), Herman Arnspiger (guitar), Wills, Smokey Dacus (drums), longtime vocalist and big part of the Texas Playboys sound Tommy Duncan, Sleepy Johnson (fiddle), Johnnie Lee Wills (banjo), Jesse Ashlock (fiddle), Joe Ferguson (bass), Al Stricklin (piano), and the definitive western swing guitar player, Eldon Shamblin.

Al Dexter, whose "Pistol Packin' Mama" and "Rosalita" were among the most popular country music records of all time. It is told of Dexter that after receiving his first record contract he had a silk shirt made up with the fancy letters "Al Dexter, Star of Brunswick Records" embroidered on the back which he wore around his hometown of Denton, Texas. (*Country Music Foundation Library and Media Center*)

unusual musical impulses, be it jazz, blues, or cajun. The group's leader, a song-writer, announcer, and flour entrepreneur named W. Lee O'Daniel, was later to use the tremendous popularity he and the Light Crust Doughboys enjoyed on radio to gain the Texas governor's chair, and eventually a seat in the United States Senate.

Vocalist Milton Brown broke with the Doughboys to form his own very popular band, the Musical Brownies, and was replaced by a singer with an appealing, mellow voice named Tommy Duncan. In September 1933 Wills, his banjo-playing brother Johnnie Lee, and Duncan split from the Doughboys to form a group called Bob Wills and his Playboys (the "Texas" was added when they moved to Tulsa), and their musical approach extended that of the Doughboys, reaching toward big-band dance style, with heavy doses of jazz on "hot" instrumental breaks. Soon to join them was another Light Crust Doughboys alumnus, a gangly teen-aged steel guitarist named Leon McAuliffe, who was to be immortalized on record by Wills' exuberant high-pitched cries of "*Aaaah*, take it away, Leon!"

Moving to Tulsa in 1934, Bob and his fledgling Texas Playboys found a perfect environment: an area starving for dance entertainment, receptive to exciting musical changes. They found as well the facilities of KVOO, a 50,000-watt radio station that boomed the sound of the Texas Playboys across millions of square miles of prairie. The popularity of the band rose explosively, and soon they were playing dances every night, either burning their way flat out across those long, straight highways or hosting a dance in Tulsa at Cain's Academy, a dancing school by day converted to a dance hall by night. They eventually became so busy, in fact, that Bob pulled his banjo-playing brother Johnnie Lee out of the Texas Playboys and formed a band around him (the magic of the Wills name) just to fill the bookings Bob was having to turn down, as well as to serve as a reserve pool of talent should a musician suddenly leave the Texas Playboys. In time two other Wills brothers, Luke and Billy Jack, were also to front their own swing bands at the height of the music's popularity.

There is a story that when Wills was first recorded by Brunswick Record Corporation in 1935 with the Texas Playboys, the session was set up on the reputation of the band alone, and the A&R man, Art Satherley, came running from the control booth in total surprise upon hearing the jazzy solos, the swinging beat, the big-band arrangements, and Bob's famous "*Aaaaaah-ha!*" from what he had thought to be just a better than average fiddle band, and was clearly reluctant to record them, thinking such a sound would never sell to rural Americans. Reminded once again of the tremendous local popularity of the band, Satherley ultimately did record them, and the success of these first records assured their longtime association with Brunswick, which subsequently became Columbia through complex legal mergers.

Satherley's reservations were justified, however, in that the basic market for "hillbilly" recordings in those days was the Southeast, which has to this day been extremely reluctant to embrace western swing. At the time he first recorded Wills, Satherley was basking in the glow of a hit record he'd produced by a young Oklahoman working out of WLS in Chicago, Gene Autry. Autry's hit song, "That Silver Haired Daddy of Mine," was a classic sentimental ballad, which, in typical southestern tradition, extolled the virtues of a home in the hills, aging parents, and a wayward son's recognition of his erring ways. It's no wonder Satherley expressed surprise at the likes of the driving "Osage Stomp" and "Get with It."

But the success of the early Texas Playboys records soon spelled out the obvious: The musical needs of the Southeast and the Southwest were dissimilar and growing more different every day. Country music, thought by the record companies for more than a decade to be the music of one region exclusively, had expanded to two regions, each with its own tastes and expectations.

As Wills' popularity, in person and on record, continued to grow throughout the 1930s, so did the size of his band, reaching a peak of twenty-two members in 1943, highlighted by four fiddles and a full brass section. Southeasterners began to think

Maybe Bob Wills' hottest band. This California version of the
Texas Playboys in 1944 or 1945 had some of Wills' most jazzy
and experimental musicians. In the back row (*left to right*) are
Jack McElroy (the announcer), Joe-Blow Galbreath (Bob's
bodyguard), Billy Jack Wills, Rip Ramsey, Millard Kelso, super
yodeler and first Texas Playgirl Laura Lee, and Tommy
Duncan. In the front row are Noel Boggs, the jazzy fiddle team
of left-handed Joe Holley and right-handed Louis Tierney, Bob
Wills, and the hot guitar duo of Jimmy Wyble and Cameron
Hill. (*Bob Pinson*)

There is no trademark in country music more immediately
identifiable than Bob Wills' exuberant *"aaaaah-ha!"* This live
shot from a 1946 dance gives some idea of Bob's constant
motion and playfulness on stage. Trumpeter Alex Brashear
waits his turn while Billy Jack Wills plies the bass, announcer
Cactus Jack smiles, Tommy Duncan looks off into the crowd,
and Junior Barnard plays a hot solo on the guitar. (*Bob Pinson*)

of them as hopelessly pop, indistinguishable from any of the the big bands of the era (an attitude supported by their highly arranged version of "Big Beaver" and the later version of "Maiden's Prayer," performed à la Benny Goodman). However, even cursory listening to a few big-band records in comparison with Wills' records of the era, while revealing the strong influence of the big dance bands—and it must be remembered that the Texas Playboys were always essentially and basically a dance band—also reveals an uncompromising rural feel: a devotion to lovelorn lyrics, continued heavy use of the steel guitar, and Bob's unending succession of wise-cracks, asides, and "aaaah-ha's." These elements lent just enough informality to be reminiscent of the country dances the Texas Playboys continued to play year after year as the staple of their income. No matter how "big band" the sound became, his avid listeners in the Southwest knew he was still just Jim Rob Wills, a good ole boy from Turkey, Texas, working out some good new dance stuff with that band of his. They simply loved him all the more for his flashy suits, $200 boots, and hot dance band, for they knew, and always he made sure to let them know, that he was still very much one of them.

World War II had its effect on western swing, as it did on all phases of American life. Besides decimating his band (even taking Bob from the helm for a little over a year), it changed America's tastes, habits, and expectations. Even though the postwar years were the biggest financially for western swing, the beginning of the end of this musical fad was becoming apparent.

Pee Wee King and his Golden West Cowboys in the early 1940s. Pee Wee became the King of Eastern Swing with his big cowboy band and pioneered the sound on the Opry when he came there in 1937. Some notable band members: San Antonio Rose is the girl singer, Cowboy Copas is standing on the far *right*, and kneeling on the *left* is Redd Stewart, who coauthored with King several of the all-time great country music songs: "Tennessee Waltz," "Bonaparte's Retreat," and "Slowpoke." (*Country Music Foundation Library and Media Center*)

Paul Howard and His Arkansas Cotton Pickers were the foremost exponents of western swing on the Opry in the 1940s, but even Howard left the popular barn dance, finding much more work for his swing band in the Southwest. (*Country Music Foundation Library and Media Center*)

Tulsa was Johnnie Lee Wills' town after brother Bob took the Texas Playboys to the West Coast, and Cain's Academy was where the dancing action took place in Tulsa. Here Johnnie Lee, who led popular swing bands for years, is presented a new Hudson Commodore. (*Bob Pinson*)

Spade Cooley's western swing band in 1944, being introduced by pioneer record producer Art Satherley. On the bass at the far *right* is Tex Williams, who was to become a million-selling singer (with "Smoke, Smoke, Smoke") for Capitol Records in years to come. (*Country Music Foundation Library and Media Center*)

It was at around this time that, interestingly enough, western swing moved east of the Mississippi, establishing a slight toehold, but never even beginning to approach the popularity it enjoyed in the Southwest. One early eastern group directly influenced by Wills and Milton Brown was the Tennessee Ramblers (led by Dick Hartman and later by Cecil Campbell), who first recorded for Bluebird in 1935. Pee Wee King had brought his Golden West Cowboys to the Grand Ole Opry in 1937, and while they worked primarily as a show—as opposed to dance—band, they incorporated a good deal of western swing into their sound: dramatically so in comparison with the old-timey mountain fiddle bands that had reigned at the Opry since its inception in 1925. Later, a solo singer on the Opry formed a band that was to develop into the closest thing to western swing east of the Mississippi. The only thing it lacked was drums, an instrument the Opry wasn't to allow on its stage for years to come. He was Paul Howard, and it wasn't all that unusual by the mid-1940s to have Howard sign off his Opry show with a Wills classic, "Miss Molly," and hear King open his set with "Take Me Back to Tulsa."

But western swing was never to catch on in the Southeast; again, the needs were not there. King's band, although swing oriented, was first and foremost a show band, replete with girl yodelers, comedians, and featured vocalists, of whom Eddy Arnold was one. The Golden West Cowboys played virtually no dances. Howard's Arkansas Cotton Pickers was really the only western swing dance band on the Opry, but dancing—of the type so commonplace in Texas and Oklahoma—was practically unheard of in the Southeast. Even Wills himself, accustomed to crowds of thousands in towns no bigger than flyspecks on the map of Texas, drew only a few hundred per dance during his 1944 southeastern tour. In 1948 King left the Opry for a lucrative television tieup in Louisville, and by the next year Howard too had left, heading for a southwestern dance circuit. The area the Opry covered, for whatever reasons, did not accept or need cheek-to-cheek dances, dance halls, or western swing.

During the postwar years Wills worked out of California with great success. Leon McAuliffe, after piloting throughout the war, formed his own band, the Cimarron Boys, and shared the Tulsa area with Johnnie Lee Wills. And the star-crossed Spade Cooley, who dubbed himself ringingly if inaccurately as the King of Western Swing, formed a huge band of over twenty pieces, with full string sections and even a harp. These were the big financial years for western swing, and the proliferation of bands and dance halls was rapid; yet the handwriting was already on the wall, and it forecast the decline of this unique musical style.

Tastes change and needs change, and Americans, generally more sophisticated after the war, were growing weary of the dreamy lyrics of "San Antonio Rose" and "Faded Love." While Wills was canny enough to move with some of the changes (the ramifications of his 1948 hit "Bubbles in My Beer" will be discussed in chapter 11), the big-band era, both for Wills and for his pop counterparts, was rapidly becoming a thing of the past, and Wills was forced to rely more and more heavily on his longtime vocalist Tommy Duncan to provide the "new" kind of songs rural America was buying.

Hank Thompson and the Brazos Valley Boys in the early 1960s. Thompson, while continuing to front a big, basically western swing band, has had continued success in contemporary country music.

But more than the taste of rural America had changed, and this was a large part of the problem. Both soldiers returning from long overseas duties and displaced southerners who had come north to work in the industrial plants of Detroit, Pittsburgh, and Chicago and stayed on after the war because of high wages felt somehow rootless, aimless. For the soldier, postwar America was not the nation he had left. For the worker in the auto plant, acres of brick, concrete, and glass were no substitute for the rolling hills or flat prairies of home. For far too many postwar Americans, alcohol was solace, and that, combined with their jaded desire for more honest—if often sentimental—expressions of real life in their music, caused the sudden popularity of songs of inebriation, of honky-tonkin', and of slipping around.

Western swing's decline, like that of the big bands, was swift; highly talented musicians suddenly found themselves out of work, their skills and ideas considered out of date, their "sound," individually and collectively, old-fashioned. It is true that there were and still are pockets in the Southwest where dance halls and small western swing bands (such as Hoyle Nix' West Texas Cowboys in Big Spring, Texas) survive but by the mid-1950s the music was for all purposes dead. The need was no longer there.

It should be mentioned again, however, that country music fans are loyal above all else, and that Bob Wills was able to continue performing (albeit at times with just a vocalist and house band) until a series of crippling strokes, which began in 1969, undermined his health. Although he was able to record as late as December 1973, it was from a wheelchair, adding only his "aaaah-ha's" to the performance of others. Following that session Wills lapsed into a coma that lasted until his death on May 13, 1975, just at the time when the music in which he'd played such an important part was beginning to be resurrected; just as interest was beginning to grow; just as the jaded tastes of American youth encouraged a search for a new "old" sound and many were finding it in western swing.

It's hard to pinpoint just where and when interest in western swing began to develop among the urban rockers and folkies. Certainly their interest parallels, a decade later, the urban love affair with bluegrass. A group that came on the bandwagon early, Commander Cody and his Lost Planet Airmen, have two band members who were deeply involved in old-time country music before branching out into fifties rock, modern coutry, and eventually swing. A band that has at the same time a more serious approach and a more consistent swing sound is Asleep at the

Wheel, who feel strongly that they are crusaders, bringing western swing to a whole new audience. While they are occasionally a bit tongue-in-cheek in their attitude toward country music in general, their zeal and musicianship cannot be faulted. They may be forerunners for some developing but undiscovered full-fledged swing band of the Wills type, or they may themselves grow into the role. Even Austin, Texas, that haven of underground country music, harbors other bands of this type in its spacious bosom, with such unlikely names as Alvin Crow and the Pleasant Valley Boys, Marcia Ball and the Misery Brothers, or the parody country swing act Kinky Friedman and his Texas Jewboys.

The strangest thing about Asleep at the Wheel and similar bands, however, is the circumstances in which they frequently play: fashionable "listening rooms," college concerts and auditoriums, all far removed from the hot, smoky, crowded dance halls where the Texas Playboys made their living night after night. This environment may demonstrate that the new audience for western swing possesses great sophistication and appreciation of musicianship as they sit listening intently through a version of "Take Me Back to Tulsa," but the full flavor of the original is simply not present without hundreds of booted and ginghamed dancers doing the two-step on a crowded hardwood floor.

Another group that has benefited enormously from the blossoming revival is, ironically, some of the Texas Playboys themselves: a group of "original" members from the early 1930s such as Smokey Dacus—Wills' first drummer and the first in country music—Leon McAuliffe, and pianist Al Stricklin, augmented by later Playboys of the late 1940s and early fifties such as the fiddle duo of Johnny Gimble and Keith Coleman and a rich-voiced singer in the Tommy Duncan tradition (Duncan died in 1967) named Leon Rausch. It was they who recorded that final album ("For the Last Time"), with Wills participating from a wheelchair. In addition, ex-Playboys mandolinist and fiddler Tiny Moore has become a full-time member of Merle Haggard's big, frequently swing-oriented band. And the man who set the style in classic western swing rhythm guitar playing, Eldon Shamblin, is a part-time member of Haggard's Strangers, as is Johnny Gimble.

Predictions are always risky and usually foolish; it is safe to speculate, however, that there is at least the possibility that western swing will come into its own once more, much as bluegrass did a decade ago. There exist the same kind of devotion to a charismatic "founding father" and the same degree of attention to the details and intricacies of musicianship that set the bluegrass fan apart from the large majority of country music fans.

Here again, however, needs must be filled. There must be a need for this music among a sufficient number of people (as there was with bluegrass) before western swing can take off again, and if the needs—and they must be far different now from those of 1938—exist today, western swing could bloom again, reaching far more people than it ever did in its prime.

The return of ballroom dancing, the nostalgic revivals of some of the big bands for tours, the hunger of American youth for alternate musical styles—these could all be harbingers of good times to come for the music of the prairie and the dance hall.

9
GOSPEL MUSIC
"Will the Circle Be Unbroken?"

If there is any one of country music's roots that might be called a taproot, a long, thick, deep root from which essential nourishment has been drawn by nearly every branch and leaf of the tree, then that root would have to be gospel music, or church music, or old-fashioned hymn singing. Call it what you will, no musical experience is more widespread in the lives of those who have created and continue to create country music than singing in small country churches, often without an instrument to guide their voices. It is a common denominator for nearly every country singer who ever appeared on stage and one that unites the whole of country music as a sound and as a musical feeling.

So many commonplace elements of country music are directly traceable to the small, weather-beaten old churches and to the earnest hymns sung there: the love of harmony singing, the use of added ornamental grace notes, the pounding rhythm of the piano, the heartfelt approach to singing, the ever-present need for a country song to have "feeling." No matter whether they were raised in the hills of Kentucky, the plains of Missouri, the prairies of Texas, or even the rolling grasslands of Pennsylvania, very nearly every country singer or musician possesses a background in church singing and grew up with generally religious and often musical parents or grandparents in or near the household, to further reinforce the bedrock religous foundation of their lives and attitudes but also to encourage the singing and playing of hymns.

In fact, religion has always been of supreme importance in the lives of the people who have been most influential in carrying on the tradition of country music and developing the sound of the music. The settlers who moved to the New World between 1740 and 1840 were, by and large, seeking the freedom of worship that our constitution is so careful to guarantee. Repelled by the turns established churches in England, Scotland, and Ireland were taking, middle-class and lower-class Protestants flocked first to the Colonies and later to the newly formed United States to

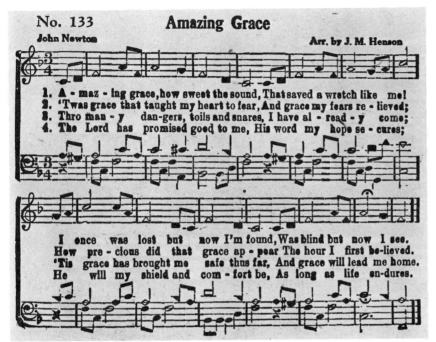

A page from a shape-note hymnal: The shape of the notes guided the voice of the singer, kind of a shortcut that made learning to sight-read music unnecessary and that became immensely popular in rural areas after the turn of the century due to the Vaughan and Stamps-Baxter singing schools.

find a haven where they could worship as they pleased. The newcomers were, however, generally disappointed to find a strong church hierarchy as stiff and class-conscious as the ones they had left behind, and consequently these Baptists, Methodists, Quakers, and Moravians were forced to take their religious preferences into the mountains and out to the edge of the frontier in a continuing search for religious freedoms. With the American Revolution, the power of English churches evaporated, leaving these backwoods, mountain, and frontier groups—ever splintering and forming new sects—to grow and spread in complete freedom, a freedom that led to the rise of intense, exciting, emotional contexts: tent meetings, camp meetings, and brush arbor meetings.

The camp meetings were closely centered around the process of being saved, being "borned again," while brush arbors, as they came to be called, were communal meetings of the poor and the deprived, a conscious social distance removed from the class-oriented established churches. With the coming of the Industrial Revolution and the rapid growth of cities, there occurred, oddly enough, a parallel rise in the popularity of fundamentalist, or "old-time," religion. It seemed that with the increasing complexity of life, there were great numbers of people—primarily rural, agrarian people—who turned to fundamentalist religion to assuage their fears about the incomprehensibly rapid changes taking place in their lives and the lives of their friends and kin. These were the people who were "saved" at tent meetings and camp meetings, who centered their entire social and intellectual life around the church, its functions and activities, and who often derived their greatest worldly pleasure from its music. It is among these same people that country music was at first preserved, then developed.

Because of the huge geographical distances involved, many rural families were virtually isolated from their neighbors or from towns, and consequently from both churches and organized religion in general. To serve these people and hundreds of tiny churches and congregations scattered throughout the South and West, two organizations sprang up within two decades after the turn of this century that had as their goal the bringing of Christian religion, in the form of sacred song, to the far-flung rural peoples of America. The James D. Vaughan organization and the Stamps-Baxter singing schools and publishing company sent out hymnals and teachers (who would stay but a week or two in any given area, much like circuit-riding judges or preachers, who were nonmusical forbears of this kind of activity) to bring the text and the music (both in shape-note [see photograph on page 145] and in conventional note form) of the fine old hymns and some excellent new ones to rural congregations. Both firms had tremendous impact on the voices and minds of youngsters who would within a couple of decades start country music on its gradual rise in commercial popularity.

It was around the time country music began to change from a tradi-tional/nostalgic art form to a creative, commercial art form that something of a division took place among both its performers and its fans as to the "proper" method of reaching people with the message of hymns and religious songs. Most country music performers of the era—Roy Acuff is a perfect example—featured a quantity of religious and semireligious music, either interspersed throughout a program or presented in a clearly designated section, much as Porter Wagoner or Lester Flatt does today: "Now it's time in our show where we sing a few good old-fashioned hymns. . . ." But another set of performers preferred to sing sacred music exclu-sively and formed quartets who sang vocal parts straight out of Stamps-Baxter songbooks, usually accompanied by a piano only, the instrument most frequently found in small country churches (if, indeed, the congregation could afford an in-strument at all). Thus began the two traditions in gospel music that are so very unalike today yet that originated, basically, from the same sources.

As early as the early 1940s, the Grand Ole Opry featured groups such as the John Daniel Quartet, and the National Barn Dance, in turn, had its Maple City Four. Yet these groups and groups like them generally found their mixed (that is, secular and sacred) repertoire uncomfortable, for a hard core of extremely religious listeners would have no truck with worldly music at all. Before long several quartets like the Blackwood Brothers, the LeFevre Family, and the Speer Family were making good livings—better, in fact, than the majority of country bands—playing in churches for donations and selling bibles, songbooks, souvenirs, and records out of the back of a car or bus. By now this branch of sacred music has grown to such a degree that it considers itself an entirely different entity from country music. It possesses its own promotional/trade organization, the Gospel Music Association; there is a Grand Ole Gospel Time on WSM in Nashville; and plans are afoot to build a Gospel Music Hall of Fame.

Anyone who has ever witnessed one of the all-night sings (like huge package shows) or "dinner-on-the-grounds" shows at local churches can immediately sense the difference between the modern, commercial gospel music show and the average country program: slick, well-barbered, flashily dressed men and women, all smiles

John Daniel, leader of the Opry's first gospel group, the John Daniel Quartet.

and hairdos and doubleknits, belting out strident songs of faith and salvation between pitches for albums and souvenirs they've brought along. To the outsider this often seems shallow and offensively commericialized, far from the spirit of sacredness the occasion seems to demand. Yet for thousands upon thousands, more so today than ever before, the music provides a genuinely moving experience, a source of hope, inspiration, and spiritual uplift. What seems to the outsider as garish and tasteless appears to the devoted gospel music fan as simply a continuation of a tradition that has been a long time in the making, and fans will accept what may seem crass if the strong, powerful religious message remains.

It is interesting to reflect upon the reasons gospel music fans—to confine the term gospel to all-sacred performances by all-sacred groups—are so adamant about their style, so determined to keep it separate, safe, and secure from the wordly influences of country music. Perhaps the attitude is an atavistic holdover from the days when musicians were considered unsavory and untrustworthy; or perhaps it harkens back to a time when the fiddle was considered by some to be the "Devil's instrument." It was, after all, over some time and with great reluctance that stringed instruments such as guitars and basses were accepted in gospel quartets, the outstanding exception being the Chuck Wagon Gang. Whatever the reasons, gospel music is in a world of its own, and despite its common origin with country music, its current sound, style, performance, and musical objectives are far different from those of country music. It is paradoxical that the musical forms are at once removed and yet rather close to the origins from which they both grew.

The Florida Boys Quartet. It was years before string instruments were accepted by gospel quartet fans, and while the piano is still the predominant instrument, guitars and basses are now finding their way into the sound.

The Chuck Wagon Gang, one of the longest-lived gospel quartets, pioneered the use of the guitar (hence the cowboy, or chuck wagon, image) in sacred music, inspiring thousands to follow them into this field.

Meanwhile, sacred country music has been and continues to be a very important part of country music, both in live performance and on record. As far back as the Carter Family's 1927 recordings there has existed a strong emphasis on religious songs as an integral part of recorded and performed repertoire. For example, of the total number of songs recorded by the Monroe Brothers, nearly half (twenty-eight of sixty) are hymns and religious songs. While they are not commonly thought of as a religious or gospel group at all, the Monroes' most successful record before they split up was "What Would You Give in Exchange for Your Soul?" In fact, this sacred/secular combination was rather typical of the repertoire of southeastern "hillbilly" bands, both that earlier era and to a lesser degree today, as exemplified by Porter Wagoner.

Despite the fact that singing cowboy Eddie Dean started his career with the James D. Vaughan Quartet, and Roy Rogers' religious sentiments are well publicized and widely known, the preference for including many religious songs in a band's or singer's repertoire is primarily a southeastern trait; certainly none of the western dance bands performed religious music, except, perhaps on very rare occasions. The same rock-ribbed religion that prevented western dance halls from becoming popular in the Southeast also assured that southeastern performers—Roy Acuff, Mainer's Mountaineers, the Carter Family, and Monroe Brothers—would present a quantity of religious material in person and on record.

It is interesting to note that there has been relatively little crossover between the fields of what is now called gospel music and that of sacred country music, although some conversions have been dramatic: Stuart Hamblen, rough-riding, hard-living

The Louvin Brothers, Ira (*left*) and Charlie, on the Grand Ole Opry in 1955, around the time they forsook straight gospel singing for a wide range of heartfelt country material, much of it, like their gospel songs, written by Ira. (*Charlie Louvin*)

Johnny Cash is one of the few who is able to successfully walk the line between gospel and secular country music, pleasing fans of both. He is shown here with his wife, June, on a recent Grand Ole Gospel Time performance. (*Grease Brothers*)

Timeless Skeeter Davis, whose first hit, "I Forgot More Than You'll Ever Know About Him," dates back to 1953. Devoting more and more of her life to religious song and work, she was suspended from the Grand Ole Opry for nearly a year (1974–1975) due to unkind remarks about the Nashville Police Department's handling of a troupe of Jesus freaks holding a makeshift revival in town. (*Little Richie Johnson*)

Diminutive Connie Smith, described as "cute and country" not so very long ago, has gone into religious music in a big way in the last few years, although she still maintains an identity among country music fans. (*Grease Brothers*)

West Coast cowboy, was converted at a Billy Graham crusade and went on to work in churches during the past twenty-five years, during the same period writing "This Ole House," "It Is No Secret What God Can Do," and other religious classics. Molly O'Day, at the threshold of what appeared to be the first successful solo career as a woman singer in country music, renounced all worldly songs and took up gospel singing exclusively. T. Texas Tyler is yet another example, as is Tim Spencer, one of the founders of the Sons of the Pioneers. There are probably hundreds more, but it is important to realize that this occurrence is still not uncommon: Skeeter Davis, Johnny Cash, and Connie Smith have all undergone highly publicized conversions during the past few years, and doubtless we'll see many more in coming years.

It is at least as interesting a phenomenon when the reverse occurs. When a primarily gospel singer or group integrates secular music into its repertoire or moves over to straight country music in a big way, the results are unpredictable. For

Martha Carson, one of the all-time greats in gospel music, shown here at her peak in the middle 1950s. She was never able to regain her momentum after a fling with country pop.

example, Martha Carson, the undisputed queen of the gospel music world in the early 1950s (her biggest hit was "Satisfied"), decided midway through that decade to become a big-time singer. Her gospel fans, horrified by her "desertion from the fold," rejected her completely; country fans found her far too slick and uptown for their tastes; and the pop market wasn't too interested in her big, exuberant style, so beautifully suited to exhortative, soul-saving gospel music. Her career withered and died, never to rise again.

On the other hand, the Louvin Brothers, despite some early secular records, rose to popularity as Capitol Records' gospel duet, with records like "Weapon of Prayer" and "The Family Who Prays" making the charts and earning them a spot on the Grand Ole Opry. They too "went country" in the mid-1950s, despite dire warnings against the move, but brought the same sincerity, emotion, musicianship, songwriting talent, and harmony singing to country love songs as they had to religious material and became a great success. Similarly, the Jordanaires began as a gospel quartet in the standard mold before becoming an essential element of the recorded Nashville sound in the late fifties and providing Elvis Presley vocal backup on record, on film, and on the road.

Molly O'Day in 1946. She was the first to record Hank Williams' songs but later turned her powerful, emotional voice to gospel music. Her producers for Columbia, Art Satherley and Don Law, called her the greatest female country singer of all time.

ROCKABILLY, COUNTR
COUNTRY ROC
COUNTRY UNDERG
"Blue Sue

The Oak Ridge Boys, the slickest, most uptown, most daring of all modern gospel groups. Their flashy dress, long hair, and appearances in Las Vegas horrify some segments of the gospel world while convincing others that the music has finally come of age.

Reverend Jimmie Rodgers Snow, who turned to the ministry after an unsuccessful attempt at following his father Hank's footsteps in the music business. Pastor of a church north of Nashville that is attended by several popular country singers, Snow is also host of the Grand Ole Gospel Time on WSM. (*Grease Brothers*)

Rock and roll: swiveling hips, juvenile delinquency, rebel beat, hot rods, rumbles, motorcycle gangs, sneering at adults Rock and roll was all this and much more to an entire g parents and was doubly threatening to those musicians, si nessmen who suddenly found themselves unneeded, unwan rock revolution affected pop, soul (then called rhythm an fields of music as well, but the music that had the most diffi (yet, paradoxically, to which so many rockers of the 195 country music.

For all its seeming blandness when compared with th decade that followed, post-World War II America was a p turmoil. Young men and women, weary of war and the parents, suddenly finding their age group a significant perce for the first time, eagerly sought something that would vi feelings of rebellion—something with all the trappings of independence and novelty, something that would upset a association, but something involving little real risk to then local country band in Pennsylvania tapped this mood in t began incorporating a few popular rhythm-and-blues num Sure enough, the audience couldn't get enough of these tun and the Comets were put on record, the result was an avala driving, pulsing new sound, with its insistent beat anc "safe"—sensuality. Black rhythm and blues, boogie-woo related styles had been around for some time, of course touched the edges of middle-American consciousness. Ha Clock," however, was somehow less gritty, less dangerous

So the switch from sacred to secular singing, although looked upon with opprobrium within the world of gospel music, can be successful. Certainly the temptation is easy to understand, for the financial rewards available in country music are greater today than ever before. In fact, the world of gospel music is presently abuzz, with the Oak Ridge Boys doing popular and country material mixed with their gospel songs, and the Blackwood Brothers playing the fleshpots of Las Vegas with Elvis. The heavy rock beat of the Oak Ridge Boys (or Oaks, as they now prefer to be called) has a strange and worrisome sound to some of those aged, die-hard fans who grew up listening to the John Daniel Quartet. Gospel music itself, however, is mushrooming at a rate at least as great as that of its secular cousin, country music, and so there obviously exists a need that this music is somehow filling, and it is a need that continues to grow.

At least for the present, religion still plays a large part in the lives of the mainstream fans of country music: It is a bedrock to which they cling in troubled times,

COUNTRY ROOTS

and if the troubles of today are inflation, layoffs, and mortgages rather
failure, hailstorms, and disease, the need for a faith is still as strong amo
as it was among their parents and grandparents. Whether the preference
gospel music or for hymns sung with sincerity by country singers, religio
rural origin is a very large though often overlooked aspect of country m
American life, for it provides hope for tomorrow and comfort for toda
and warm tradition rooted firmly in the past.

The early Elvis. This quivering, gyrating, mannered but
moving product of Sun Records delighted millions of American
youths while intimidating and threatening their parents.

154

Bill Haley, whose "Rock Around the Clock" both named and initiated a gigantic musical trend, rock and roll. Long the leader of a minor Pennsylvania country band, Haley was the first to blend black rhythm with white voicing and started the avalanche that looked for a time as though it would bury all other American musical forms, country music included.

The still popular Everly Brothers as they appear today, although they have broken up their long-standing duet to pursue solo careers, a fate not uncommon among brother groups who find a lifetime of close personal contact uncomfortable.

pretty bland fare to our jaded modern ears, it provided a safe way for thousands of young whites to enjoy the power and excitement of this new music, to obtain thrills from flirting with the unknown, and to adopt as a thing of their own a music their parents would not and could not understand and enjoy.

If rebellion played a big part in the rock revolution among young record buyers, so did it with rock's performers, who, in surprisingly large measure, were country boys simply finding a new way of letting off steam. In fact, most of the early white rock and rollers, despite their adoption of much of the language and inflection of the black rhythm-and-blues sounds they sought to emulate, were those very musicians one would expect to seek careers in country music (as, indeed, most of them originally had). They were white, southern, (with the notable exception of Haley), lower- or lower-middle-class, undereducated but talented youngsters seeking an escape from their environment through music. Though hardly associated with rock, Charlie Louvin expressed the sentiment well for all struggling young musicians of the period: "We were hunting something easier than the cottonpatch and the cane fields."

The origin of the word *rockabilly* follows close on the heels of the term *rock and roll* itself, for Sun Records, by far the most influential label in the genre, began describing the energetic fusion of black and white sounds they specialized in as "rockabilly" as early as 1955. Sam Phillips, who started the label primarily for rhythm-and-blues recordings, had a musical vision: a white singer who could adopt the jump, the boogie, the blues of black music yet sing it convincingly, with more raw "guts" than the bland but enormously popular Bill Haley, who had changed the name of his band from the Saddle Pals to the Comets, reflecting his own growing association with rhythm and blues and the rock and roll he was creating.

Phillips soon found the artists he was seeking in a surly-looking but disarmingly polite Memphis youngster named Elvis Presley, and in the son of a sharecropper from Jackson, Tennessee, named Carl Perkins, who combined a Hank Williams-like vocal style with a heavy rock beat and an exciting, sputtering guitar style. It was Perkins' record of "Blue Suede Shoes" that put Sun and the music called rockabilly on the map. Presley and Perkins were later joined by two other young men who were to become tremendously important in both rock and country music: rough-edged Johnny Cash and wildly flamboyant Jerry Lee Lewis ("and his pumping piano," as the Sun labels often added). These four, whom Sun called their Million Dollar Quartet, eventually, of course, made many times that amount. Their music was high-energy, intense, perfectly suited to the strange dancing techniques that were developing, and it possessed that magical union Sam Phillips so desired: the excitement, drive, and tension of black rhythm and blues combined with the sincerity and straightforwardness—as well as the white "safeness"—of country music. These four were later joined, albeit briefly, by a trio of other singers and musicians who were to make deep impressions in both fields of music: Roy Orbison, Conway Twitty (who recorded for Sun under his real name, Harold Jenkins), and Charlie Rich, country/soul sensation of the 1970s, who was a studio pianist and occasional recording artist at Sun for several years.

Elvis with the two musicians who did more than anything to shape his sound: Scotty Moore (*left*), a legendary rockabilly guitar player, and Bill Black, the bass player. Black died in the early 1960s, while Moore is active as a producer in Nashville today. Although the trio was originally to split earnings 50%-25%-25%, Moore and Black wound up making $250 a week salary when Elvis hit his first peak.

The careers of the Million Dollar Quartet are fascinating to follow, for the four rock and rollers who so definitively styled rock music in the middle and late 1950s have come back, to greater and lesser degrees, to country music in recent years. Presley, who still brings untold millions into RCA coffers yearly, has done the least returning to country roots; certainly he is under no economic incentive to return, although he has recorded a country album ("Elvis Country") in recent years, and his records are regularly charted on the country, as well as pop, hit list. Perkins, whom many consider to be the definitive rockabilly singer and guitarist, had difficulty getting his career restarted following a serious auto accident, but survived stormy bouts with pills and alcohol* to become a popular and welcome addition to the current country music scene, writing, recording, and bringing his exciting rockabilly style to millions as a member of Johnny Cash's road show. The big hit record still eludes Perkins, however, despite his legendary status among rock historians. Cash himself, of course, survived much of the same kind of self-inflicted damage** to emerge as one of country music's greatest and most enduring stars and spokesmen. Although popular in all fields with Sun and later with Columbia, he seems always to have considered himself primarily a country singer with some pop following, and of all the Million Dollar Quartet has maintained the strongest continuous ties with country music. Certainly he personified all that was country music to millions in the late 1960s through his ABC television show; it was an image he cultivated quite

---

* Colin Escott and Martin Hawkins, *Catalyst: The Sun Records Story* (London: Aquarius Books, 1975), p. 44; Christopher Wren, *Winners Got Scars Too: Life of Johnny Cash* (New York: Dial Press, 1971), p. 77.

** Escott and Hawkins, *Catalyst*, pp. 165, 191–192; Wren, *Winners Got Scars Too*, pp. 131–133, 143–144, 149–150, 157–162, 165, 181–193.

Charlie Rich, "The Silver Fox." He wasn't so silver when he began as a studio piano player for Sun Records in the late 1950s, and while everyone claimed he was destined for big things, it took him nearly two decades to finally get that hit—"Behind Closed Doors." Rich's revue today is far from the gritty Sun Records sound, but he's doing fine in Las Vegas. (*Mercury Records*)

Elvis at the piano with the Jordanaires, a former gospel quartet, *oooohing* and *aaaahing* in the background, as they did in his movies and on his records for years. They are (*left to right*) Gordon Stoker, Hoyt Hawkins, Neal Matthews, and Hugh Jarrett. (*Country Music Foundation Library and Media Center*)

consciously. Jerry Lee Lewis's erratic personal life (which included his furor-arousing marriage to a thirteen-year-old cousin) finally forced even the outwardly rebellious 1950s rockers to shun him, with heavy moralistic overtones. He eventually reappeared on the country music scene in the late 1960s with a series of exuberant country recordings like "What Made Milwaukee Famous Made a Loser Out of Me." Lewis continues to be a popular country performer today, his somewhat tamer stage antics more a nostalgia trip than a threat to middle-class morality.

It is difficult to gauge with any accuracy, but the "Sun Sound," or "Memphis Sound," developed by Sam Phillips at Sun has had a significant effect on all aspects of American music. Rough, expressive, heavy on echo and sparse in instrumentation, the sound was more of a feel than anything, and few copied it with any success, including the Million Dollar Quartet, none of whom ever sounded the same after moving on to bigger labels. In addition, Sun provided an impetus for many established country singers to try to adopt the new sound, because of its instrumental similarity to the makeup of their own bands—an experiment that was occasionally successful but just as often embarrassing. The Million Dollar Quartet also provided inspiration for scores of up-and-coming country musicians who wanted to keep abreast of the times in the framework of their tradition.

A case in point: The Everly Brothers, a pair of young Kentuckians associated in no way with Sun Records or its famous sound, were developed as a traditional country duet. Along the lines of a younger Louvin Brothers, their unique, rhythmic guitar style and songs of teen-age woes ("Wake Up, Little Susie," "Bird Dog") had them perched high atop all charts in the late 1950s. From a singing family (their father, Ike, possessed a celebrated finger style on the guitar not dissimilar to that of

"Great Balls of Fire" tore the rock world apart when it was released and helped make Sun Records the rock legend that it is. After a few years in obscurity, "The Killer," as he affectionately calls himself, came back and became an extremely popular country singer. Jerry Lee Lewis is tamer on stage than he was, but he still tears up a crowd. (*Mercury Records*)

Two rockabilly legends as they appear today: Johnny Cash and Carl Perkins. Both have survived intense personal difficulties to regain some of their former popularity. Cash is now probably at the height of his career and is becoming something of a spokesman for country music on a national level. Perkins, who tours with Cash's road show, says, "I figure I went from low to high to just about the middle. That's an advance, isn't it?"

The first publicity photo of the Everly Brothers, Don and Phil, shortly after they began recording. Produced and promoted as a country act, their intense harmony and unique rhythm made them tremendous overnight successes in rock and even in what was then called rhythm and blues as well. (*Country Music Foundation Library and Media Center*)

Merle Travis), they were pure country in background yet became classic rockabilly singers. Perhaps the most interesting facet of their story is that they were marketed for their first several releases as pure country; it was only after a couple of huge across-the-board hits that any effort was made to preserve and promote the rock identity they had established basically by accident.

Although the Everly Brothers were exceptional, country artists who didn't utilize the fabled Memphis Sound developed at Sun also occasionally made big waves in the pop field: Marty Robbins, with "A White Sport Coat and a Pink Carnation," a lament about being stood up for the prom; Sonny James, with "Young Love";

ROCKABILLY, COUNTRY-FOLK, COUNTRY ROCK, AND COUNTRY UNDERGROUND

Johnny Bond, with "Hot Rod Lincoln"; and Johnny Horton, with "The Battle of New Orleans" and "Sink the Bismarck."

The rebellious, nose-thumbing cockiness of rock and rockabilly did not appeal to all teen-agers of the 1950s, however. A smaller but still influential group of young men and women took an alternative route in expressing their alienation from and dissatisfaction with the lives their parents led. Largely a northern, urban trend, the so-called folk-song revival had a national impact on country music, changing it both from without and within.

The exploration of folk cultures for their intrinsic worth inevitably led a certain group of urban adventurers to delve into mountain folk music and by extension into old-time string bands, bluegrass, and eventually, for some, more modern country music. As the folk boom developed, there occurred the inevitable cross-pollenization, with young country singers like George Hamilton IV and Bobby Bare adopting the roles of country folk singers. Likewise, young folkies like Jerry Garcia (now of the Grateful Dead), Steven Stills, John Hartford, Linda Ronstadt and the Nitty Gritty Dirt Band adopted (occasionally) what they'd learned in their earlier days and spread it to the rock audiences they played to in the late 1960s and early 1970s. At that time both country music and what came to be called country rock began to proliferate, spearheaded by groups such as the Byrds and the Flying Burrito Brothers, and later Poco, the Eagles, the New Riders of the Purple Sage, and is

Little Brenda Lee started out as a child singer on the Ozark Jubilee, which was hosted by Red Foley. As an early teen-ager she had great success in the rock field, although some of her stuff was good rockabilly: "Sweet Nothin's" for example. Still a young woman, she has recently resumed recording country material. (*Country Music Foundation Library and Media Center*)

Running contrary to the heavy instrumental trend in country music is Sonny James, who usually appears just as shown, with three singers, a bass player, and his guitar as the only lead instrument. Although his first hit "Young Love," was in the pop field, James has remained firmly in the realm of country music ever since, running up a tremendous string of number-one records. (*Country Music Foundation Library and Media Center*)

A leader in the country-folk movement among country musicians, Bobby Bare first scored with that moving ballad "Detroit City," which expresses the spoken and unspoken longing of millions of displaced, homesick southerners. Still popular, he is shown here with his son doing their rendition of his recent popular record, "Daddy What If?" (*Grease Brothers*)

George Hamilton IV started out with a rock hit, "A Rose and a Baby Ruth," but quickly adopted the country-folk genre as his own when it came along. Immensely likeable and articulate, he has introduced country music to numerous foreign countries, most recently Russia. With him is Loretta Lynn, who escaped a life of grinding poverty as a miner's daughter in Butcher Hollow, Kentucky, to become the leading female country singer of today.

typified by the emergence of Linda Ronstadt as a country/pop star of major proportions.

This process is involved but has happened so frequently among headliners and side musicians alike that it is familiar indeed: A restless but talented youngster picks up a banjo or mandolin or guitar as an alternative to both his parents' preference for Lester Lanin's Orchestra and to the drippy strains of mediocre pop/rock, which he hears among his peers. Here he finds a fresh, exciting music that is real, earthy, quaint, evocative of another era, yet dignified in a shy but stubborn way. Better yet, the banjo, mandolin, or guitar are instruments from which some pleasing or at least intriguing music can be coaxed with only a few hours of diligent practice, opening up a new and exhilarating world of musical knowledge. This initial interest may broaden or narrow to a single style such as bluegrass or old-time music, but our youngster listens to a lot of radio as well, and the music of Bob Dylan and the Beatles is as much a part of his musical makeup as is that of Charlie Poole or the Stanley Brothers. This broad musical interest eventually leads to a flirtation with what is often called "straight" country music (often picked up from Jimmie Rodgers or Hank Williams). Often, however, the music is simply parodied, and little of the respect held for the folk ancestor of the commercial music is carried into "straight" country. The flirtation is little more than a fascination provoked by gaudy sequined stage suits, Hank Williams stories and songs, and a somewhat morbid interest in the crass and tacky side of Nashville. Still pop songs and styles are infused into this music, and soon, if the youngster is good, country-flavored but pop-rock-oriented music is being written and performed.

This is the saga of a surprisingly large number of important figures in popular music today and forms the life story of hundreds of band members, sidemen, and aspiring pickers and singers in Nashville and on both coasts. The importance of this saga is not the music that was ultimately developed—it occasionally hits very high points, though they are all too rare—but is instead the worldwide exposure given country music by these groups, who presented it as a worthwhile and charming part of American life to a world hungry for such cultural information.

It is in this regard that a word must be said here about a figure who has been dominant in American music for well over a decade. Bob Dylan, in his own unique way, had a dramatic effect on country music, not because of the adoption of a good deal of his repertoire—that has not happened—or because of his success in the field, which, in terms of popularity with country audiences, is limited indeed. Rather his tremendous effect has been as an influence that somehow encouraged creative young musicians to write as well as play and sing, and scarcely one of the young singer-songwriters who make up the majority of the country hitmakers of the last few years has been unaffected by the influence cast by Bob Dylan. The creative end of country music—which, in terms of songwriting, has been increasingly the most vital facet of all modern music business as the pop scene continues merely to develop the new blandness of the 1970s—owes an enormous debt to Dylan's inspiration.

Although rock and folk were heavily influenced by country and country music was influenced by both folk and rock during the past two decades, the fields were

A collection of country music heavyweights who gathered to record the "Will the Circle Be Unbroken" album with the Nitty Gritty Dirt Band. *Clockwise*, beginning with guitarist, they are Jimmy Fadden of the NGDB, Doc Watson, Merle Travis, Pete "Bashful Brother Oswald" Kirby, Earl Scruggs, and Vassar Clements. (*Country Music Foundation Library and Media Center*)

(and are) rather distinct and separate, although vague gray patches obscure boundaries, making rigid definitions and examples impossible and pointless. Nevertheless, two new and unique phenomena have been taking shape in the very recent past: one direction has been taken by a loose group of bands lumped under the heading of southern rock. To a large degree, groups like the Charlie Daniels Band, the Marshall Tucker Band, and to some extent the Allman Brothers, are not unlike the Sun-sound rockabillies of two decades ago: synthesizing southern blues and country music (with twenty years of rock history to further influence their sytle), they are young working-class musicians producing their own kind of music, neither intellectualizing it on the one hand nor changing it to keep up with some slick and ephemeral standards on the other.

Listen to the Charlie Daniels Band's "The South's Gonna Do It Again," an explicit and highly chauvinistic glorification of this movement and its members—its boogie beat and twin guitar lead are more than a little reminiscent of Bob Wills' experiments with boogie of thirty years ago and more.

While much of southern rock is indeed "hard" rock, there is much of country music in this movement, and, in historical terms, it is far less radical for country

Waylon Jennings ca. 1970. Successful in Nashville as a straight country singer, he was among the vanguard that grew uncomfortable with the inherent strictures and was one of the first to become a leader in the country underground movement. (*Country Music Foundation Library and Media Center*)

With "I'm Not Lisa" Jessi Colter stepped out of the role of the Wife Of Waylon Jennings Who Also Sings to that of Popular And Talented Star. She's not a strong singer, but she has the abilities as a songwriter and producer to sustain her early success. (*Capitol Records*)

music of our day than Elvis and Carl Perkins were for the country music of twenty years ago.

The other, rather opposite movement—but more comprehensible to country music's mainstream—is a strange and energy filled convergence of folk/rock musicians, singers, and songwriters who have come to country life for their inspiration and to country music for a musical base on which to build their own individual styles. These new talents have combined with creative, dissatisfied genuine country musicians who revere the roots of their music yet who feel the Nashville scene is too slick, too "big business," too aesthetically confining, and too commercial. It has been happening—and it is such a recent phenomenon as to be still embryonic—in the middle-sized, middle-American, middle-Texas town of Austin, the latest, hippest place to be in the music business.

Austin, after all, has attracted the likes of Jerry Jeff Walker and Michael Murphey on one hand, "cosmic cowboys" who discard their upbringing by adopting the role of semicountry singer, cowboy, and down-home (yet trenchant) philosopher and sage. On the other hand there are singers like Waylon Jennings and Willie Nelson, authentic country singers who, despite success and acclaim in mainstream country

Willie Nelson in his Nashville country singer days, mid 1960s. He seems to have been as uncomfortable in that Nehru jacket as he looks. Since moving to Austin, Texas, he has blossomed as a creative artist and songwriter, although several of his earlier songwriting efforts are true classics, including "Night Life" and "Gee Ain't It Funny How Time Slips Away." (*RCA Records*)

Kris Kristofferson: Rhodes Scholar, songwriter, actor, singer, helicopter pilot, former RCA janitor. His struggle for success in Nashville is a classic story of the down-and-out songwriter making good through persistence, and he now has a host of songs to his credit that will remain country music standards for years to come. (*Country Music Foundation Library and Media Center*)

music, became highly publicized country music "outlaws": hard-living, bearded good ole boys who sang the praises of Lone Star beer and created some of the most unusual, energetic country music of the past decade. The two forces have combined to form what is often described as country underground, and if some of it is a bit tedious and self-indulgent, much of it is the most exciting and involving music ever to have developed from country roots. A mixture of cowboy chauvinism and ethereal poetry, of western swing and progressive pop, of Texas dancehall classics and new songwriters' creations, it is as varied in quality and in excitement as its performers.

It still is, of course, much too early to assess the effects on country music, of what might be called, loosely, the "Austin Sound," since as a movement it has not yet begun to reach full flower. It seems, however, a healthy thing for country music, and, in the light of history, an inevitable evolution. Progressive underground music exists in all our musical forms, and it was only a matter of time before some restless musician, resisting the confines of convention (always of some strength in country music), would seek to stretch boundaries and develop individualistic ideas within the loose framework of traditional country music.

Two shots of Willie Nelson today, the creative leader of the country underground movement. Based in Austin, Nelson is, after long years, getting his share of artistic appreciation. (*Grease Brothers*)

With the increasing urbanization, suburbanization, and musical sophistication of the ever-broadening American middle class, it appears inevitable that much of the future of the music we revere as country music will come from the inspiration of those considered outlaws a few years ago and defined as underground today. Whether it is spearheaded in Austin, or Nashville, or Memphis, or Denver, or Dubuque, this is very much a music of the future. It will not suppress other elements of country music—no fad has yet been strong enough to do that—but it will, to a large extent, determine much of what will be called country music a decade from now. Creative new country music is happening everywhere, and good traditional country music is simultaneously available on a national and even international scale. But keep your eyes on the Lone Star State—there is something going on down there in the land of the armadillo that will have important consequences in coming years for all of us who love country music.

II
HONKY-TONK, COUNTRY POP, AND THE NASHVILLE SOUND
"Bright Lights and Country Music"

The years following World War II were times of tremendous social upheaval, and nowhere was this reflected more dramatically than in the business and creation of country music. The post-Depression 1930s, our age of innocence and good-natured charm, came to an abrupt end with the bombing of Pearl Harbor, and when war-weary veterans returned home from overseas, it was realism they sought in entertainment, not fantasy; a reflection of life as they'd come to know it all too graphically, not a replay of those entertaining escapes into fantasy that had helped this country pull itself out of that Great Depression.

This loss of innocence was soon reflected in country music, a bellwether always quick to respond to gut feelings of social change. Prewar "hillbilly" songs dealt cautiously and indirectly with sexuality and infidelity (except for some of the remarkably explicit lyrics of several of the blue yodels of Jimmie Rodgers and his troupe of imitators) in terms of "left me for another," "don't forget me," "proved untrue," or "I'm losing you" and the like. But not too long after the war powerful songs that touched an exposed nerve began to appear, expressing the pain and anger of infidelity, separation, and divorce.

Similarly, the attitudes reflected in prewar music toward drinking, toward carousing, toward hanging around in smoky honky-tonks, as they were to be called, were ones of complete opprobrium and disapproval, whether suggested humorously, as in The Dixon Brothers' "The Intoxicated Rat," or with gruesome moralistic overtones, as in Roy Acuff's "Wreck on the Highway," in which "whiskey and blood run together" over a wreckage-strewn pavement. Though these attitudes were indicative of country music's traditional reliance upon the values of rural America, harking back to the ideals (never to the realities) of an earlier era, by 1950 this reliance had begun to weaken.

Trends in the music's treatment of sex and drinking were accurate barometers of the changing American social climate, and the early years of the postwar period,

Ernest Tubb's record shop on a Nashville Saturday night. (*Grease Brothers*)

more than any other era in country music, present a picture of a time, a place, and a society coping with wrenching changes and dealing with those changes as best it could.

As early as 1942 a song that reflected, ahead of its time, the anguish displaced southerners were to experience during the war and postwar years was Ted Daffan's million seller "Born to Lose." The first-person narrative of a young man who has "lived my life in vain," the song provides an intense sketch of severe emotional pain experienced at the end of a romantic relationship. To millions who heard it, however, "Born to Lose" became by extension much more than this, eventually earning status as a national anthem for the displaced mountain and prairie youth who had journeyed to Detroit or Cleveland or Flint or Chicago or Los Angeles to find work during the war years and had remained in the city, too changed by its way of life to return to the country yet not sufficiently adapted to enjoy urban life. The undereducated, often ill-nourished southerner frequently felt hopelessly trapped by these wages and this way of life in impersonal northern and far-western cities, locked into an existence that promised a barren future of hard-spent days, hard-drinking nights, and little chance of personal betterment. With too little back home to prompt return, and making too much money to leave the city, he increasingly turned to drink as a way to wipe out the seemingly insoluble problem rather than face it. This was the focus of a similar song, popular two decades after the end of

Ronnie Milsap is one of those extremely talented singers and musicians about whom everybody in the industry says, "It's only a matter of time before he hits." Ronnie finally hit with Kris Kristofferson's "Please Don't Tell Me How the Story Ends" and was the Country Music Association's Male Vocalist of the Year in 1974.

World War II: Bobby Bare's "Detroit City." It is a firsthand account of a homesick southerner locked into this cycle of working and drinking: "By day I make the cars, by night I make the bars."

The "Born to Lose" syndrome is laced with heavy overtones of guilt as well, for despite the honky-tonkin' life the displaced farm youth might come to accept, there remain still the strong memories of strict, religious, but aging parents who would disapprove if only they knew; of a church where promises were made to God that have long since been broken; and of a land of natural beauty and freedom. These thoughts prey on and revolve in his mind; no matter where he turns, he can't win, and the song on the jukebox, "Every dream has only brought me pain . . . Born to lose, and now I'm losing you," has a special, powerful, evocative meaning, reaching far beyond the overt message of lost love it conveys.

"Born to Lose" was, for a time, the theme song of the displaced countryman and may well be one of the few landmark songs in the history of country music, for it expressed emotions that infused a whole way of life for a substantial portion of our population at one unique moment in the history of the United States. Fulfillment, in terms of the classically defined Middle-American Dream (two cars, suburban home, etc), may be too readily at hand today for the song to mean much anymore, but in its day nothing was more precise or more evocative of the homesick, work-weary southerner torn from his roots.

Ted Daffan, despite the picture, played the steel and fronted Ted Daffan's Texans, a band best known for Daffan's timeless compositions (written under the pseudonym of Frankie Browne): "Worried Mind," "No Letter Today," and the song that so captures the frustration of the rural American facing the unexpected and bewildering pressures of urban life, "Born to Lose."

Hank Williams, a genuine country music legend.

Because music, particularly country music, does reflect life, it's difficult to pin-point a specific time or place where trends begin. In the case of "cheatin' " songs, however, the harbinger of change seems to have occurred around 1946 or so, when a tall slender singing cowboy named Eddie Dean, his wife, Lorene "Dearest," and Hal Blair wrote a song called "One Has My Name, the Other Has My Heart." Phrased in romantic generalities, the song nonetheless placed marital infidelity right out front without apology, only with regret ("If I could live life over . . ."). Unable to interest a major label—explicit infidelity was an unwritten taboo among radio broadcasters, and no one at that time was willing to break that taboo by taking a chance on the song—Dean was nonetheless convinced of the song's potential and recorded it for a small West Coast label called Crystal over the heated objections of the company's owner. Although Dean personally promoted the record heavily, disc jockeys still wouldn't play it, explaining at length that such songs just could not be played over the radio.

Capitol Records remembered the song, however, and by the next year had sensed the shifting public mores in the wind. They took a chance on it, doing a version with another smooth-voiced singing cowboy, Jimmy Wakely. "One Has My Name" was a smash hit, and the era of the cheatin' song had begun. The harmony singer, un-credited on Wakely's version, was a prominent big-band vocalist named Margaret Whiting, singing as part of an experiment she and Wakely had worked up. The results, in terms of vocal match and harmony, were superb, and in 1949 the two recorded Floyd Tillman's classic cheatin' song "Slippin' Around," which became a quick million seller, and an early country crossover that sold heavily in pop markets.

The effect of these West Coast efforts was not lost on the more conservative Southeast (remember the West Coast had enjoyed popular dance halls for well over ten years, something still relatively uncommon in the South of 1950), and Ernest Tubb, for example, was quick to cover "Slippin' Around" for Decca.

From that point on the comparatively explicit cheatin' song became firmly en-trenched in country music's repertoire and in fact for a few years was the dominant story line used in country music. Webb Pierce, famous for his silver-dollar-encrusted car and flashy Nudie's of Hollywood suits, is but one of many hundreds of singers who began to make their living and their mark in association with songs like Pierce's classic, "Back Street Affair." Another such example is Hank Thompson, who sang of the lure of both cheap whiskey and wild women in "The Wild Side of Life."

In fact, these two prevailing themes—illicit love and the honky-tonk life—were gradually to become inextricably entwined, and it wasn't long before the image of one conveyed the other in the public mind. Drinking and slipping around were part and parcel of the serious and widespread postwar malady, and country music of the era reflected America's preoccupation with those very sensitive areas.

Again, the drinking songs, the honky-tonk songs, proliferated on the West Coast, where wartime crowds had packed ballrooms and dance halls to drink and dance to Bob Wills, Spade Cooley, and other big western swing bands. Wills' 1947 recording

Informal shots of Hank Williams are rare. Here is one of him entering a dressing room before a show in the early 1950s. (*Bob Pinson*)

Hank Williams, Jr. Despite numerous tribute, duet (electronically superimposed), and "standing in the shadows" songs and albums, Hank Junior has a style and a stature of his own and has earned his place in country music on the strength of his own talents, although serious injuries sustained in a recent fall while hunting has put a crimp in his career. (*Country Music Foundation Library and Media Center*)

The early Ray Price, ca. 1955. At first a protégé of Hank Williams, Price fused Williams' southeastern feel with the western swing influence he'd grown up with in Texas to make one of the most popular and influential sounds of the 1950s. Forsaking his "Cherokee Cowboy" image in the late 1960s, he became a leader in the tuxedo-clad country-pop movement with "Danny Boy" and "For the Good Times." (*Country Music Foundation Library and Media Center*)

of "Bubbles in My Beer" is expressive of the change in morals, for rather than condemning or ridiculing the protagonist's honky-tonkin' ways, it simply presents a portrait of a defeatist ("I know that my life has been a failure . . .") approach to solving problems: soaking up suds in a honky-tonk. Of course it had long been a common occurrence in life, but here it was at last dealt with in song, and another unwritten rule was brushed aside by changing American tastes and expectancies. Actually, this trend had been foreshadowed before the war with songs like Al Dexter's "Honky-Tonk Blues," but it was the big bands that brought the problem to the forefront of American consciousness.

Again, the more conservative Southeast began to pick up on the best-selling cues from the West Coast, and before long Hank Williams' lonesome voice was shouting the joys of "Honky-Tonkin' " while simultaneously crying over "Your Cheatin' Heart." It was Hank—then a honky-tonk singer, today a legend—and Ernest Tubb who brought this music, redolent of smoky roadside taverns and tightly pressed dancers, to full flower on the Grand Ole Opry and throughout the Southeast.

Ultimately it took a young protégé of Williams to fuse the two regional styles, creating a unified country sound appealing to both coasts and the Southwest as well. The artist was Ray Price, born and reared in Texas, who absorbed the music of Bob Wills in his youth yet who aspired to develop a vocal sound like Hank Williams —with whom, in fact, Price had roomed for a time when both were young and down on their luck in Nashville. His early records, in contrast to the heavily vibratoed, mellow-voiced Price we know today, were nearly twins to those of Williams vocally, but a crucial difference was discernible in the overall music of Ray Price: the twin-fiddle, Texas two-beat shuffle sound that backed him up. His string of hits continued through the 1950s and 1960s, including, significantly, songs accepting with resignation the life of the honky-tonker ("Night Life") and the stolen pleasures of extramarital affairs ("Release Me"). These themes were to reign unchallenged in country music for over a decade.

The sound of Webb Pierce was the sound of country music for a time in the middle 1950s: His high-pitched, tightly vibratoed voice somehow carried a message America was ready to hear, and it took Sonny James a decade and a half to break his string of over twenty number-one records in a row. Today Webb Pierce is a wealthy businessman who rarely finds time to perform, but this shot from the middle 1950s shows him at his peak as a country singer, preparing for a show.

The undisputed master of the truck-driving genre (though Dick Curless or Red Sovine might argue the point with some justification) is big, rough Dave Dudley, a native of Wisconsin who summed up the romance of the open road with "Six Days on the Road."

Ernest Tubb, the Opry's first honky-tonk singer, and one of his finest bands: (*left to right*) Jack Drake, Dickie Harris, and the great Billy Byrd, one of the first country guitarists to delve into jazz.

Hank Snow, originally a disciple of Jimmie Rodgers, became Canada's Yodeling Ranger for a few years before emigrating to the United States, where huge hits like "I'm Movin' On," "It Don't Hurt Any More," and "You're the Reason I Don't Sleep at Night" propelled him to stardom on the Grand Ole Opry. His 1974 number-one record, "Hello Love," prompted RCA to extend his contract to a length which will total fifty full years with the firm. (*Grease Brothers*)

Stonewall Jackson's story is legendary: He pulled up to the Opry in a log-hauling truck, auditioned, and was immediately signed to the Opry without a single hit record or even a record contract. The Opry's confidence was justified, however, when Stonewall wrote his way into country music history with such hits as "Don't Be Angry" and "Waterloo." (*Grease Brothers*)

If there are two constants in country music, the first is that it is a sensitive music, exceedingly quick to pick up on the sentiments of a great number of people and to express these sentiments for the millions all over the world who are too inhibited, unreflective, or inarticulate to express emotion for themselves. At the same time, however, it is a music of tradition, of fierce loyalty to past musical styles, which accounts for the tremendous diversity of sound (although not always so evident in radio where a top-twenty or top-forty syndrome is dominant) within country music through the years. No matter what style or fashion is currently the most popular, there remains demand for all the subgenres of country music. So although the honky-tonk and cheatin' songs began to grow a bit wearisome in the late 1950s (assaulted by the thundering waves of rock and roll), they have remained an important and continuing category of country music repertoire, as witnessed by songs like Tammy Wynette's "D-I-V-O-R-C-E," which still become extremely popular despite the use of a shopworn theme.

An interesting sidelight in country music history was the short-lived vogue for historical songs that appeared in the late 1950s, such as Marty Robbins' gunfighter ballads and Lefty Frizzell's "Saginaw Michigan." The undisputed master of this narrow style, which hearkened back to the saga songs of an earlier era, was Johnny Horton, a honky-tonk singer who affected both country and pop fields with "The Battle of New Orleans" and "Sink the Bismarck" before his untimely death in an automobile accident in 1960. The historical song appeared as yet another effort to fight the devastating effects of rock and roll, which had by that time knocked the

Carl Smith had a fantastic string of hits in the early 1950s, including "I Overlooked an Orchid," "Deep Water," and at least a dozen others. Though he's not the record seller he once was, he's still popular, and he's shown here indulging in his second love: gentleman farming on his spread near Franklin, not far outside of Nashville. (*Grease Brothers*)

Bill Anderson. "Whispering Bill" is no threat to Jim Reeves as a singer, but his success at songwriting is so phenomenal as to be almost legendary: He's written hits for just about everybody, starting with Ray Price's "City Lights" in 1959 and continuing to this day. No matter when you read this, check the latest *Billboard*, and it'll be a rare occasion if a Bill Anderson song or two isn't on the country charts. (*Grease Brothers*)

Lefty Frizzell had one of country music's truly great and original voices: rich, slurring, a little corny but always intensely moving. Lefty was one of a kind, a genuine original, and although he'd not had a hit in some years (his early-1950s feat of having four songs in the top ten simultaneously has yet to be duplicated, however), he was a solid and steady record seller. He was once again blooming as a songwriter when he died suddenly and totally unexpectedly of a stroke at the age of 47 in 1975. More than a few people think Lefty was the greatest country singer ever.

wind out of country music. Although this type of song generated a number of hit records, it was only a relatively brief, if fascinating, musical trend.

A longer-lived—and currently thriving—trend is country pop, a style, if it may be called that, which has been around almost as long as commercial country music: Vernon Dalhart's 1925 recording of "The Prisoner's Song" was nationally popular and was the first country song to sell a million records. Jimmie Davis' "You Are My Sunshine" was to have a similar pop music impact in the 1930s. Both Gene Autry, with his smooth vocal style joined with orchestral accompaniment, and Bob Wills, offering his Texas version of the big dance band, had enormous influence in spreading a more nationally popular approach to country music, even as the mournful brother groups and the Carter Family were still in their heyday in the Southeast.

If there was a king of the historical song genre, it was surely Johnny Horton, who had enormous success in the late 1950s with "The Battle of New Orleans," "Sink the Bismarck," "When It's Springtime in Alaska," "North to Alaska," and "Johnny Reb." He moved from the Louisiana Hayride (where this shot was taken in the mid-1950s) to the Grand Ole Opry shortly before his death in 1960 in an automobile accident. (*Country Music Foundation Library and Media Center*)

Ageless and perennially popular Marty Robbins has done it all: pop rock ("A White Sport Coat and a Pink Carnation"), pop country ("This Time You Gave Me a Mountain"), western ("El Paso," "Big Iron"), Hawaiian ("My Isle of Golden Dreams"), country blues ("Shotgun Daddy"), Caribbean ("Devil Woman"), and pure, sweet, all-time great country: "I Never Felt More Like Singin' the Blues" and "Don't Worry 'Bout Me."

Billed early in his career as the "Tennessee Plowboy," Eddy Arnold shed that image in the process of becoming a smooth, popular media star, introducing country music to huge television audiences in the 1950s. He is shown here in the early 1950s with legendary country guitarist Hank ("Sugarfoot") Garland and longtime accompanist Little Roy Wiggins.

Red Foley was one of the handful of rich-voiced country-pop pioneers of the late 1940s and 1950s. Although he never sought to forsake his country image, his full, controlled baritone voice won many fans who were not attracted to Roy Acuff or any of the other mountain singers. Foley seemed comfortable with any material: He's often remembered for the saccharine "Old Shep," yet won a gold record for "Chattanoogie Shoe Shine Boy," and was one of the rare few who placed a hit record in the top ten with a religious song, "Peace in the Valley." Shown with him in this early-1950s Opry appearance is Ernie Newton, the original and long-popular bass player who was among the first session musicians when Nashville started to become a recording center. (*Country Music Foundation Library and Media Center*)

Barriers really began to fall in the late 1930s, however, when Bing Crosby recorded a series of hits with a rural air or western flavor: "Don't Fence Me In," "Mexicali Rose," "Sweethearts or Strangers," and the million-selling "San Antonio Rose," also a million seller for Wills. Crosby's crooning embracement of some elements of country music style or repertoire was to have a broad effect, for several country singers, realizing Crosby was reaching a market that was potentially theirs, began to smooth out their own vocal styles, deliberately trying for a mainstream approach. Out west, Jimmy Wakely, although firmly identified as a singing cowboy in film, sang in a voice not unlike Crosby's. And back east a member of Pee Wee King's Golden West Cowboys named Eddy Arnold obtained a recording contract with RCA on the strength of his smooth vocal style, and by the mid-1950s Arnold had established an identity in the pop field that completely overshadowed his earlier "Tennessee Plowboy" billing. Arnold's appeal has been so broad and timeless that he has earned continuous success with crossover hits from the late 1940s to this day.

Interestingly, Arnold's replacement as a featured vocalist with the Golden West Cowboys was the band's fiddler and guitarist, another young singer in the smooth pop style named Redd Stewart, who with King was to write such country classics as "Bonaparte's Retreat," "Slowpoke," and the all-time top-money grosser in country music, "Tennessee Waltz."

Meanwhile from the other end of the musical spectrum, pop music's infiltration of country music continued during Arnold's biggest years, and such pop singers as Patti Page, Tony Bennett, and Guy Mitchell were not infrequently seen on pop charts with versions of country material—much of it from the pen of Hank Williams—arranged for voice and orchestra. The overall effect of this pop infiltration was very subtle. It did not benefit country singers or writers all that much at the time, in terms of either financial or reputational rewards, and even for song publishers (frequently Acuff–Rose), some of whom may have enjoyed popularity for a time, the financial rewards were not that great (with the exception, of course, of "Tennessee Waltz"). But although immediate gratification was by and large not there, the occasional crossover did have the effect of continuing the trend that Autry and his fellow singing cowboys had begun: the de-yokelization of the country song among non-country fans. The seeds of acceptance among a wide public were beginning to sprout, slowly but surely paving the way for the nationwide acceptance of the country music that was to come.

Nashville in the late 1950s was a place of both manic creativity and gloom. Rock and roll had the business foundering in waters in which it was far from secure, yet copius creative energies were being developed, nowhere to a greater degree than among a group of adventurous country musicians who created, first in clubs and later on record, the subtle musical feeling that has come to be called the Nashville Sound, a loose, slightly jazzy, interpretive feel that began to appear on records in the late 1950s. Spearheaded by the multi-talented musician/producer/executive Chet Atkins, a number of other musicians with interests ranging from country into pop and jazz helped develop this sound, including guitarist Grady Martin, pianist

Sexy Jean Shepard first had a hit as a teen-ager, with her 1953 Korean War classic, "Dear John," and later in that decade scored with "A Satisfied Mind." Now a longtime member of the Grand Ole Opry, her 1974 number-one record, "Slippin' Away," once again demonstrated the tremendous loyalty of country music fans.

Gentleman Jim Reeves. His smooth, relaxed, yet moving voice would have made him a star in any field, yet while he extended the boundaries of country music toward middle-of-the-road pop, he nonetheless carefully maintained his image as a country singer. More than a decade after his death in a small plane accident, his name still sells records consistently, especially overseas.

Don Gibson was another of those cherished and highly polished Nashville stories: Everybody thought he had the makings of a big star—his talent was obvious—but he bounced around from company to company before finally scoring with a fantastic string of hits in the mid-1950s: "I Can't Stop Loving You," "Sea of Heartbreak," "Blue Blue Day," and many others. He's still having big hits: 1973's "Woman, Sensuous Woman" was a number-one record for him.

Three men who helped shape the so-called Nashville Sound to an enormous degree. Chet Atkins (*left*), tremendously influential as both a guitarist and a producer, saxophonist Boots Randolph (*center*), and pianist Floyd Cramer, whose "slip-note" piano style has become synonymous with country music.

Floyd Cramer, drummer Buddy Harmon, bassist Bob Moore, and the legendary Hank Garland, a country boy from South Carolina who was only barely beginning to reach his full potential as a jazz guitarist before a near-fatal auto accident in 1963 cut his career short.

Another attribute of the Nashville Sound was "voices," the "*ooooh-aaaaah's*" in the background, the use of which apparently has become nearly mandatory in current recording practice. A former male gospel group called the Jordanaires (most famous for their work with Elvis Presley) and another group headed by a former WSM staff employee, the Anita Kerr Singers, picked up most of this work originally, but demand has grown to such a degree that Nashville studios currently use several similar groups. A smooth, extremely subtle blend, "voices" have added much to the Nashville Sound, although occasionally their indiscriminate use has hammed up otherwise superb records—Lefty Frizzell's "Saginaw Michigan" comes to mind.

It was this sound and this style that helped keep Nashville alive during the rock-and-roll years and thereafter, for while the 1950s and the early 1960s weren't easy going by any means—particularly for the musically traditional bands and singers—compared to the woes of the music business in general, the country field was a place of creativity at work in an era of experimentation and even of a little profit.

If these changes seem, in retrospect, to have occurred with bewildering speed, sentiments were very similar at the time: Singers, songwriters, businessmen, all were terribly confused by the rapidity of change in public taste, and their groping, hit-or-miss methods of reacting to these changes reflected not only the temper of the music industry of the era but also the confusion of all of what we have of late tended to call middle America. For this was the beginning of America's age of self-reflection, self-examination; an era that openly doubted assumptions and values that had previously been accepted without question; an era that sought with fervor to correct ills that had festered for so long; an era riddled with doubt of the past but full of optimism toward the future. It was a time that questioned the validity and honesty of the commercial aspects of the music business and performance, and while one large segment of the American audience sought musical integrity in the purity of folk music, another sought rough honesty and raunchy sensuality in rock. Both groups tended to idolize performers—the folkies for their social concern and dedication, the rockers for their sassy nose-thumbing at both authority and commerciality—while, for the most part, conveniently ignoring the commercialism inherent in any professional performance.

It was an era of change, of doubt, of grasping and groping, all reflected in country music's fragmented tangents. Yet the young musicians who grew into country through either folk or rock—and they are legion—were to make a deep impact on the direction the music was to take, through their desire for musical forms both traditional and experimental.

It would be unrealistically romantic to view this new generation of country musicians as single-handedly bringing country music back where, in their eyes, it belongs, for changes had actually begun from within. Again, as often has been the case, it was western influence that brought back both the fiddle and the steel guitar (and with them a sense of return to the traditional) to country music in the early-to-middle 1960s, a reawakening of tradition apparent on, for example, such Buck Owens records as "Together Again." Western swing musicians, always in the country music vanguard, had taken the steel guitar so far along the road of hot jazz in the hands of such men as Buddy Emmons and Speedy West that it was simply much too far out for the average listener with limited musical knowledge. On the other hand, the stereotyped "licks" of eastern steel players were hopelessly passé and reminiscent of a "corny" image deplored by the increasingly suburban listener. Owens, on his early records, featured a modern, mellower steel-guitar tone, combining it with something of the plaintive, crying feeling of old-time steel guitar. It was largely through the efforts of Owens' pedal steel man Tom Brumley—now with Rick Nelson—that mainstream country music was made understandable and evocative once more, and it wasn't very long at all before rock groups such as Poco,

Buck Owens struggled for years as a studio guitarist before getting a break as a singer, and his early records, "Excuse Me (I Think I've Got a Heartache)" and "Together Again," are some of the finest country music ever recorded. Lately he's begun to sound a little like a parody of himself, but he's still experimenting, still growing, while running a multimillion dollar enterprise out of Bakersfield, California, and hosting "Hee Haw." (*Capitol Records*)

The hits George Jones and Tammy Wynette have had individually and together are seemingly endless. Both have contributed greatly to their individual styles and have influenced many who have followed—ever notice how much Johnny Paycheck and a half-dozen other semipopular country singers use George's famous closed-mouth technique and his way of bringing his voice up and down in volume like a pedal steel?

What can you say about Merle Haggard in a couple of sentences? He's got the talent, as a singer, musician, and songwriter; he's got the sensitivity; he's got the consistency; he's got the greatest country-swing band in the world; he's got the respect for tradition to record tribute albums to Jimmie Rodgers and Bob Wills. It may well be that we're fortunate enough to be contemporaries with one of the all-time greats. Here he is the year he won all those Country Music Association awards (1970).

After years of making a great living as a studio guitarist, Glen Campbell burst onto the country music scene in the late 1960s as a powerful vocalist with such songs as "By the Time I Get to Phoenix," "Wichita Lineman," and "Gentle on My Mind." Leaning strongly toward the pop end of the spectrum, Campbell nevertheless maintains a strong country identity (which his television show was always careful to do), and his records continue to sell in both markets. A phenomenal musician, he has, in the last couple of years, taught himself to play the bagpipes, which he did on his recent country hit, the old Pee Wee King-Redd Stewart classic "Bonaparte's Retreat." (*Capitol Records*)

Charley Pride, a native of Sledge, Mississippi, who adopted the Hank Williams sound as his own. His race was at first a hindrance then a help to his career. He is now being accepted on his merits as a singer and entertainer alone, which is, of course, as it should be. (*Country Music Foundation Library and Media Center*)

Anne Murray keeps drifting back and forth between country and pop, but she's lucky in a big way that fans of both genres accept her readily. Her rich, haunting voice and faultless—if soulful—interpretation may have something to do with it. (*Capitol Records*)

Donna Fargo, a former schoolteacher from North Carolina, who, like so many secret dreamers around the country, wrote songs and fantasized about becoming a country singer. Only thing is, her dreams came true; no wonder she's "The Happiest Girl in the Whole USA."

the Grateful Dead, and Commander Cody began featuring the same steel sound in undisguised admiration.

Likewise the fiddle, which had been replaced for a time by gushy string sections in much of the music of the mid 1960s, has made a recent comeback in recording, largely due to the talents of Buddy Spicher and later the virtuoso ex-Texas Playboy Johnny Gimble. Masters in many musical styles, these men adapted fiddle playing to modern country music and have brought the instrument back from an undeserved obscurity. If string sections still bury many records, a good many others feature "hot" fiddle breaks these days, and thus the scales are balanced.

The return to popularity of these instruments indicates a feeling, a trend: If the Nashville Sound helped sustain country music through its lean years, perhaps the country music public—however increasingly suburban in makeup—felt it had moved too far, for in the mid to late 1960s a definite trend toward the traditional was becoming apparent, due, to some degree at least, to the strong, if conflicting,

Olivia Newton-John's soft, feather-light vocals and outrageously catchy songs make her records appeal to all—because of their inoffensiveness if nothing else. But it makes you wish somebody with all that talent would try something a little gutsier. (*MCA Records*)

demands of an increasingly youthful and increasingly decentralized audience. For every slick, modern-songed Glen Campbell there emerged a harsh and direct Johnny Cash; for every golden-throated Anne Murray there was a tear-jerking Tammy Wynette or a tough Jeannie C. Riley. And a singer of honky-tonk songs named Merle Haggard, who sounded like an up-to-date Lefty Frizzell, became perhaps the greatest country star of our time. In attempting to blend creative new music (he is a prolific and consistently excellent songwriter) with forms from the past (such as his tribute albums to Jimmie Rodgers and Bob Wills), Haggard has given country music a sense of living tradition, creative and successful in contemporary music. Unless I miss my guess, history may well judge him one of the greats of all time.

Johnny Rodriguez, discovered by Tom T. Hall, is not only bringing a delightful Latin sound to pure country music (listen to him sing "Born to Lose") but at last gives the teeny boppers something to drool at—something long missing from country music ranks. (*Mercury Records*)

Ten years from now you may look at this caption and say, "You mean there was some doubt at one time?" On the other hand, you may be saying, "Who?" For right now, Emmylou Harris looks to have the potential to be the first folk-rocker to step into the mainstream of country music and be accepted wholeheartedly. She has all the tools; all she needs is a couple of big records. (*Courtesy Warner Brothers Records*)

But despite this hungering for the traditional—a hungering that remains strong—there was no stopping the pop infusion. More than one Music City type has been heard to say, "The great thing of it is, we're not going to them—pop music is coming to us!" An overstatement, to be sure, but not without a gleam of truth. Both Campbell and Murray scored heavily on country charts, really trying for the market, just as John Denver, Mac Davis, Charlie Rich, and Olivia Newton-John are doing at present. They are not trying to sell to the country market as such, but their records happen to do very well there, reflecting the ever-increasing sophistication of the country music buying public.

On the other hand, country songs have been crossing over to pop with increasing frequency. Donna Fargo's "Happiest Girl in the Whole USA" is a good, though single, example. This is both good and bad, for it leads to an increasing blandness on the part of many country record releases, introduced in the hope of producing that elusive but financially rewarding "crossover" that hits in both fields. However, such recordings do, without doubt, awaken new audiences to country music.

For the music at present, this too is a time of doubt and confusion, interestingly, not unlike the floundering 1957–1960 period: Country music is making money, much more than ever before, both for the traditionalists and the pop singers who cross over into that field, but it is in search of some bright new sound to generate that fantastic across-the-board response that so rarely occurs. The words of one Music Row type seem to sum up the feeling of the entire industry: "We're looking for another 'Harper Valley PTA.'" Whether the creative forces for this future change will come from tradition (as suggested by the burgeoning revivals of bluegrass and western swing) or from the genius of one man, woman, or group is of course impossible to predict, but the music business is, paradoxically, both cyclical and unpredictable. The feeling in the air is that it is time for sweeping change. The question every Music Row businessman would give his eyeteeth to answer correctly is: From whom?

It should be an interesting next decade.

CHRONOLOGY

Including the Top Five Records, 1923–1975[*]

1877   A method of sound reproduction using a tinfoil cylinder is invented simultaneously by Thomas A. Edison in the United States and Charles Cros in France.

1885   Chichester A. Bell and Charles S. Tainer replace Edison's tinfoil with wax-coated cardboard.

1887   Emile Berliner patents the lateral-cut, flat-disc gramophone.

1889   The first commercial gramophones are manufactured by a toy factory in Germany.

1890   The wreck of the C&O train occurs near Hinton, West Virginia, which becomes the basis for "Engine 143," recorded by the Carter Family and many others.

1891   The first sale of phonographs as entertainment: nickel-in-the-slot cylinder players featuring recorded songs by famous opera singers.

1900   Casey Jones dies in the wreck of the 382 in Vaughn, Mississippi.

   The first printed use of the word *hillbillie*, in the New York *Journal*, April 23.

1903   The wreck of the "Old 97" occurs near Danville, Virginia.

1906   Victor markets the first Victrola.

1907   Lee DeForest invents the three-vacuum tube, which made radio a practicality.

1909   The height of "rube" comedy on record: long country dialect tales like "Uncle Josh" become popular.

1913   A dance craze sweeps America, contributing to a big rise in sales of phonographs and records.

1916   Aspiring light-opera tenor Vernon Dalhart's first recording.

1920   The broadcast of returns during the November 2 presidential election by KDKA in Pittsburgh is considered the birth of professional radio broadcasting.

   Jimmie Rodgers marries Carrie Williamson.

1922   First Fiddlin' John Carson, then Clayton McMichen, begin broadcasting over WSB in Atlanta.

   Eck Robertson first records for Victor Records in New York City. These are considered the first country music recordings.

[*] Since there was significant chart action for both sides of some top records, the flip side (following the slash) is included.

CHRONOLOGY

1923   Robertson is followed into the recording field by Fiddlin' John Carson, who records for Okeh in Atlanta, and Henry Whitter, who records for Okeh in New York.

WBAP in Fort Worth starts the first radio "barn dance."

TOP RECORDS:
1. "Sally Goodin' "/"Ragtime Annie"—Eck Robertson
2. "Little Old Log Cabin in the Lane"—Fiddlin' John Carson
3. "Arkansas Traveler/Turkey in the Straw"—Eck Robertson and Henry Gilliland
4. "Wreck on the Southern Old 97"—Henry Whitter

1924   Vernon Dalhart records "The Prisoner's Song," which is to become the first million-selling country record.

The WLS Barn Dance begins in Chicago, led by announcer George D. Hay. The early cast starred Ford and Glenn, Chubby Parker, and Grace Wilson.

Vocalion Records begins their Special Records for Southern States series.

Okeh Records begins their Old Times Tunes series.

TOP RECORDS:
1. "The Prisoner's Song"—Vernon Dalhart
2. "The Wreck of the Old 97"—Vernon Dalhart
3. "Little Rosewood Casket"—Ernest Thompson
4. "Old Joe Clark"—Fiddlin' Powers and Family
5. "Rock All Our Babies to Sleep"—Riley Puckett

1925   George D. Hay is hired away from the WLS National Barn Dance to become program director at Nashville's new WSM. Within months he starts a similar show, which he calls the WSM Barn Dance, with its stars—Dr. Humphrey Bate, Uncle Jimmy Thompson, and Deford Bailey.

Columbia begins their Old Familiar Melodies series.

Al Hopkins records for Okeh, and their recording director, Ralph Peer, names them "The Hillbillies" after Hopkins' classic statement "Call the band anything you want. We're just a bunch of hillbillies from North Carolina and Virginia, anyway."

Gene Autry goes to work as a relief telegrapher for the St. Louis & Frisco Railroad in Oklahoma.

Bradley Kincaid joins the cast of the WLS Barn Dance.

Victor and Columbia issue the first commercial electrical recordings.

TOP RECORDS:
1. "The Death of Floyd Collins"—Vernon Dalhart
2. "When the Work's All Done This Fall"—Carl T. Sprague
3. "Roving Gambler"—Kelly Harrell
4. "Letter Edged in Black —Vernon Dalhart
5. "Don't Let Your Deal Go Down"—Charlie Poole

1926   Formation of the Skillet Lickers—Gid Tanner, Riley Puckett, and Clayton McMichen.

Ralph Peer leaves Okeh Records; works for Victor Records without pay with the understanding that he may publish all original works that he records for Victor, thus the beginnings of the Peer-Southern Organization.

TOP RECORDS:
1. "The Dying Cowboy"—Carl T. Sprague
2. "Ida Red"—Riley Puckett
3. "Hand Me Down My Walking Cane"—Kelly Harrell
4. "Old Joe Clark"—Gid Tanner and the Skillet Lickers
5. "Little Old Log Cabin in the Lane"—Ernest Stoneman

1927   WSM Barn Dance renamed the Grand Ole Opry.

The Carter Family, the Tenneva Ramblers, Jimmie Rodgers, and Alfred G. Karnes first record for Victor in Bristol, Tennessee, the first week in August.

Wilf Carter (Montana Slim) first goes to work on radio in Canada.

Formation of NBC and CBS networks (1927-1928).

Jimmie Rodgers' recording of "Blue Yodel" (which has come to be called "T for Texas" or "Blue Yodel #1") is the first recording of the blue yodel style.

TOP RECORDS:
1. "Sleep Baby Sleep"—Jimmie Rodgers
2. "Wednesday Night Waltz"/"Goodnight Waltz"—Leake County Revelers
3. "Golden Slippers"/"My Blue Ridge Mountain Home"—Vernon Dalhart
4. "Lindbergh (The Eagle of the U.S.A.)"—Vernon Dalhart
5. "John Henry"—Gid Tanner and the Skillet Lickers

1928   Victor begins their Old Familiar Tunes and Novelties series.

Victor's recording of early Opry string bands mark the first recording sessions held in Nashville.

TOP RECORDS
1. "Blue Yodel"—Jimmie Rodgers
2. "Daddy and Home"/"My Old Pal"—Jimmie Rodgers
3. "Waiting for a Train"—Jimmie Rodgers
4. "Birmingham Jail"/"Columbus Stockade Blues"—Darby and Tarleton
5. "Bury Me Under the Weeping Willow"—Carter Family

1929   Gene Autry first records in New York.

Arkie the Woodchopper and Zeke Clements join the WLS National Barn Dance.

Jules Verne Allen named Official Singing Cowboy for New Mexico.

The Singing Brakeman, a fifteen-minute short, filmed in Hollywood. A Columbia-Victor Gem, it stars Jimmie Rodgers, who sings "Waiting for a Train," "Daddy and Home," and "Blue Yodel."

TOP RECORDS:
1. "I'm Thinking Tonight of My Blue Eyes"—Carter Family
2. "My Clinch Mountain Home"—Carter Family
3. "My Carolina Sunshine Girl"—Jimmie Rodgers
4. "Foggy Mountain Top"—Carter Family
5. "Desert Blues"—Jimme Rodgers

1930   Ken Maynard becomes the first cowboy to sing on screen in his *Song of the Saddle.*

Arthur Smith teams up with Sam and Kirk McGee to form the Dixieliners.

Bob Wills forms Alladin's Laddies, which later become the Light Crust Doughboys.

Dr. Brinkley begins radio station XER in Del Rio, Texas, with a transmitter just over the border in Mexico. Later to become XERA, the station broadcasts all over the United States with ten times the power allowed north-of-the-border stations.

John Lair and the Cumberland Ridge Runners (Karl Davis, Harty Taylor, and Red Foley) join the WLS Barn Dance.

TOP RECORDS:
1. "Lulu Wall"/"Sweet Fern"—Carter Family
2. "Frankie and Johnny"—Jimmie Rodgers
3. "I Left My Gal in the Mountains"—Gene Autry
4. "Worried Man Blues"/"The Cannonball"—Carter Family
5. "Naw, I Don't Wanta Be Rich"—Carson Robison

CHRONOLOGY

1931   Tex Ritter appears on Broadway in *Green Grow the Lilacs*.

TOP RECORDS:
1. "Blue Yodel #8" ("Muleskinner Blues")—Jimmie Rodgers
2. "Moonlight and Skies"—Jimmie Rodgers
3. "New Salty Dog"—Allen Brothers
4. "Lonesome Valley"—Carter Family
5. "Strawberry Roan"—Beverly Hillbillies

1932   George Gobel joins the cast of the WLS National Barn Dance as "The Little Cowboy."

Victor signs Wilf Carter (Montana Slim), first major Canadian artist.

Homer and Jethro band together.

Milton Brown leaves the Light Crust Doughboys to form his Musical Brownies; his replacement is Tommy Duncan.

TOP RECORDS:
1. "That Silver Haired Daddy of Mine"—Gene Autry and Jimmy Long
2. "My Mary"—Stuart Hamblen
3. "Mother the Queen of My Heart"/"Rock All Our Babies to Sleep"—Jimmie Rodgers
4. "Twenty-one Years"—Bob Miller
5. "Moonlight and Skies"—Gene Autry

1933   Jimmie Rodgers dies of tuberculosis in New York, shortly after completing his final session for RCA Victor. He is carried back to Meridian, Mississippi, by train for burial.

WWVA Jamboree in Wheeling, West Virginia, begins.

Bob Wills and Tommy Duncan leave the Light Crust Doughboys to form Bob Wills and his Playboys.

Lulu Belle joins Scotty.

Tin Pan Alley songwriter Billy Hill writes "The Last Roundup," a national hit, which helped accelerate a growing nationwide interest in western music.

Leon McAuliffe, at the age of sixteen, joins the Light Crust Doughboys.

Ken Maynard stars in *The Strawberry Roan*, probably the first of many cowboy movies to be named for songs.

Martin begins building the D-45, today the most valuable series of all-collectors' guitars (under one hundred were built). The first was a custom order from Gene Autry. Later country stars to play pre-war D-45s include Charlie Monroe, Ernest Tubb, Wilma Lee Cooper, Red Smiley, and Johnny Cash.

TOP RECORDS:
1. "Yellow Rose of Texas"—Gene Autry and Jimmie Long
2. "Peach Pickin' Time in Georgia"—Jimmie Rodgers
3. "The Death of Jimmie Rodgers"—Gene Autry
4. "There's an Empty Cot in the Bunkhouse Tonight"—Gene Autry
5. "Seven Years with the Wrong Woman"—Bob Miller

1934   Gene Autry's cameo role as a singer in Ken Maynard's *In Old Santa Fe* brings about such a tremendous public reception that he stars in *The Phantom Empire*, a science-fiction western serial, later in the year.

Bob Wills and his Playboys move from Waco to their longtime home, KVOO in Tulsa, and change the band name to the Texas Playboys.

Decca Records is formed as a 35 cent budget label.

Tim Spencer, Bob Nolan, and Len Slye form the Pioneer Trio, soon to become the Sons of the Pioneers.

TOP RECORDS:
1. "The Last Roundup"—Gene Autry
2. "Brown's Ferry Blues"—Delmore Brothers
3. "Down Yonder"/"Back up and Push"—Gid Tanner and the Skillet Lickers
4. "Beautiful Texas"—Light Crust Doughboys/Jimmie Davis
5. "I'm Here to Get My Baby out of Jail"—Karl and Harty

1935   Juke boxes begin to make their first big impact in the record industry.

Bob Wills' first recordings with the Texas Playboys.

Ray Whitley, cohost with Tex Ritter of New York's WHN Barn Dance, moves to Hollywood to sing in films. Ritter was to follow him the next year.

TOP RECORDS:
1. "Tumbling Tumbleweeds"—Gene Autry
2. "I Want to Be a Cowboy's Sweetheart"—Patsy Montana
3. "Nobody's Darlin' But Mine"—GeneAutry/Jimmie Davis
4. "Under the Double Eagle"—Bill Boyd's Cowboy Ramblers
5. "Cattle Call"—Tex Owens

1936   The heyday of duets: the first recordings of the Monroe Brothers, the Blue Sky Boys, and the Dixon Brothers.

Milton Brown killed in an automobile accident.

Roy Acuff first records "Wabash Cannonball" and "The Great Speckled Bird."

Tex Ritter moves to Hollywood.

Ernest Tubb, under the guidance of Carrie (Mrs. Jimmie) Rodgers, first records.

TOP RECORDS:
1. "Mexicali Rose"—Gene Autry
2. "Maple on the Hill"—J. E. Mainer's Mountaineers
3. "What Would You Give in Exchange for Your Soul?"—Monroe Brothers
4. "Spanish Two-Step"—Bob Wills
5. "Texas Sand"—Tune Wranglers

1937   Pee Wee King and his Golden West Cowboys join the Grand Ole Opry.

Len Slye leaves the Sons of the Pioneers to build a solo film career, first as Dick Weston, then as Roy Rogers.

John Lair and Red Foley start the Renfro Valley Barn Dance on WLW in Cincinnati.

TOP RECORDS:
1. "Steel Guitar Rag"—Bob Wills
2. "The Great Speckled Bird"—Roy Acuff
3. "Trouble in Mind"—Bob Wills
4. "Right or Wrong"/"Get Along Home Cindy"—Bob Wills
5. "Steel Guitar Blues"/"Steel Guitar Chimes"—Roy Acuff

1938   The Duke of Paducah's "Plantation Party" radio show goes on CBS network.

Ray Whitley assists Gibson guitars in designing the SJ-200, which was to become a country music classic. Soon Gene Autry, Jimmy Wakely, Tex Ritter, and others were playing similar instruments.

Roy Acuff and the Smokey Mountain Boys join the Grand Ole Opry.

The Carter Family moves to XERA in Del Rio, Texas.

The Monroe Brothers split, each forming his own band.

Woody Guthrie moves to New York, becoming a major force in bringing rural-oriented music to an urban audience.

The Columbia Broadcasting System buys control of the American Record Company (ARC) and reactivates the Columbia label.

TOP RECORDS:
1. "Wabash Cannonball"—Roy Acuff
2. "There's a Gold Mine in the Sky"—Gene Autry
3. "Maiden's Prayer"—Bob Wills
4. "Take Me Back to My Boots and Saddle"—Gene Autry
5. "When It's Springtime in the Rockies"—Gene Autry

1939   BMI (Broadcast Music Incorporated) formed to overcome the Tin Pan Alley orientation of ASCAP (American Society of Composers, Authors, and Publishers), opening the way for country—and all minority—songwriters to be assured of proper payment for their work.

Gene Autry's "Melody Ranch" goes on CBS radio network, sponsored by Wrigley's Gum. For the next eighteen years, it is a Sunday-afternoon staple of American life.

Bill Monroe and Zeke Clements join the Grand Ole Opry.

The Grand Ole Opry goes on NBC radio network: a half-hour segment sponsored by Prince Albert Tobacco, hosted originally by Roy Acuff, and later by Red Foley.

Red River Dave's performance is televised from the New York World's Fair, probably the first country music to make it to television.

TOP RECORDS:
1. "San Antonio Rose"—Bob Wills
2. "New Spanish Two-Step"/"Spanish Fandango"—Bill Boyd
3. "It Makes No Difference Now"—Jimmie Davis
4. "Sparkling Blue Eyes"—Wade Mainer
5. "Back in the Saddle Again"—Gene Autry

1940   Minnie Pearl and Paul Howard join the Grand Ole Opry.

TOP RECORDS:
1. "New San Antonio Rose"—Bob Wills
2. "You Are My Sunshine"—Jimmie Davis
3. "South of the Border"—Gene Autry
4. "Worried Mind"—Ted Daffan
5. "Too Late"—Jimmy Wakely/Jimmie Davis

1941   Bing Crosby records "You Are My Sunshine" and "New San Antonio Rose" and continues to record western and country songs off and on through the years with great success.

The Carter Family splits up: A.P. and Sara retire, Maybelle and her daughters Helen, June, and Anita reform as the Carter Family shortly thereafter.

The Grand Ole Opry moves into the Ryman Auditorium.

Billboard begins listing "Top Hillbilly Hits."

TOP RECORDS:
1. "You Are My Sunshine"/"It Makes No Difference Now"—Gene Autry
2. "I'm Walking the Floor over You"—Ernest Tubb
3. "Take Me Back to Tulsa"—Bob Wills
4. "When My Blue Moon Turns to Gold"/"Live and Let Live"—Wiley Walker and Gene Sullivan
5. "Be Honest with Me"—Gene Autry

1942   A musician's union strike ("Petrillo Ban") halts all recording activity for over a year.

The practice of awarding gold records for million-selling records began a bit earlier with a presentation to Glenn Miller for "Chattanooga Choo Choo." Country music receives it's first gold record for Elton Britt's RCA recording of "There's a Star Spangled Banner Waving Somewhere."

Spade Cooley forms his big band.

Eddy Arnold joins Pee Wee King's Golden West Cowboys as a featured vocalist.

Billboard begins an "American Folk Music" section.

TOP RECORDS:
1. "There's a Star Spangled Banner Waving Somewhere"—Elton Britt
2. "My Life's Been a Pleasure"/"Please Don't Leave Me"—Bob Wills
3. "The Honey Song"—Louise Massey and the Westerners
4. "Wreck on the Highway"/"Fireball Mail"—Roy Acuff
5. "Tweedle-O-Twill"—Gene Autry

1943   Ernest Tubb and the Bailes Brothers join the Grand Ole Opry.

Formation of Acuff-Rose, first country music publisher in Nashville, by songwriter Fred Rose and Roy Acuff.

The Camel Caravan brings country music to the troops.

TOP RECORDS:
1. "Pistol Packin' Mama"—Al Dexter
2. "Born to Lose"/"No Letter Today"—Ted Daffan
3. "Night Train to Memphis"/"Low and Lonely"—Roy Acuff
4. "Home in San Antone"/"Miss Molly"—Bob Wills
5. "You Nearly Lose Your Mind"—Ernest Tubb

1944   Bob Wills, released from the army, moves his base of operations to California.

Bradley Kincaid joins the Grand Ole Opry.

Jimmie Davis elected to a four-year term as governor of Louisiana.

Eddy Arnold first records for RCA.

Billboard introduces the first real country charts in mid-year: "Most Played Juke Box Folk Records."

TOP RECORDS:
1. "Smoke on the Water"—Red Foley
2. "So Long Pal"/"Too Late to Worry, Too Blue to Cry"—Al Dexter
3. "There's a New Moon over My Shoulder"/"Jealous Heart"—Tex Ritter
4. "Soldier's Last Letter"—Ernest Tubb
5. "You're from Texas"—Bob Wills

1945   Decca records Red Foley and Ernest Tubb in Nashville; although Victor's 1928 field trip marks the first actual recording in Nashville, it was this Decca session which signaled the beginnings of Nashville's rise to prominence as a recording center.

Rex Allen joins the WLS National Barn Dance.

Earl Scruggs joins Bill Monroe's Blue Grass Boys, completing the formation of the "classic" bluegrass band: Monroe, Scruggs, Lester Flatt, Chubby Wise, and Cedric Rainwater (Howard Watts).

Wilma Lee joins Stoney.

Hill and Range Music enters the country music publishing field, following the lead of Acuff-Rose.

The first full year of accurate country charts.

TOP RECORDS:
1. "Shame on You"—Spade Cooley
2. "You Two Timed Me One Time Too Often"—Tex Ritter
3. "At Mail Call Today"—Gene Autry
4. "Oklahoma Hills"—Jack Guthrie
5. "I'm Losing My Mind over You"—Al Dexter

CHRONOLOGY

1946   RCA Victor begins first regular recording in Nashville.

Hank Wiliams first records for Sterling Records; signs writer's contract with Acuff-Rose.

Leon McAuliffe forms his Cimmaron Boys after leaving the air force.

TOP RECORDS:
1. "Guitar Polka"—Al Dexter
2. "New Spanish Two-Step"—Bob Wills
3. "Divorce Me C.O.D."—Merle Travis
4. "Rainbow at Midnight"—Ernest Tubb
5. "Sioux City Sue"—Zeke Manners

1947   Pee Wee King leaves the Grand Ole Opry, moving to Louisville to begin a television show; by the mid-fifties he broadcasts a television show from Louisville, Cincinnati, Cleveland, and Chicago—once a week from each city.

KRLD in Dallas starts the Big D Jamboree.

Ernest Tubb headlines the first country music package show at Carnegie Hall.

Magnetic recording tape comes into limited use.

TOP RECORDS:
1. "I'll Hold You in My Heart 'Til I Can Hold You in My Arms"—Eddy Arnold
2. "Smoke! Smoke! Smoke! (That Cigarette)"—Tex Williams
3. "It's a Sin"—Eddy Arnold
4. "So Round, So Firm, So Fully Packed"—Merle Travis
5. "What Is Life Without Love?"—Eddy Arnold

1948   Columbia Records introduces the long-play album.

Hank Williams joins the Louisiana Hayride.

Mercury Records enters the country field.

Lester Flatt and Earl Scruggs leave Bill Monroe's Blue Grass Boys and soon form their own band, the Foggy Mountain Boys.

WLW Midwestern Hayride goes on television.

Bob Wills releases "Bubbles In My Beer."

Billboard renames their country charts "Best Selling Retail Folk Records."

TOP RECORDS:
1. "Bouquet of Roses"—Eddy Arnold
2. "Humpty-Dumpty Heart"—Hank Thompson
3. "One Has My Name, the Other Has My Heart"—Jimmy Wakely
4. "Tennessee Saturday Night"—Red Foley
5. "Anytime"—Eddy Arnold

1949   Hank Williams joins the Grand Ole Opry.

Rex Allen leaves the WLS National Barn Dance; he is the last of the real singing cowboys.

RCA introduces the 45 rpm single.

Billboard renames their country charts "Country and Western."

TOP RECORDS:
1. "Slippin' Around"—Jimmy Wakely and Margaret Whiting
2. "Lovesick Blues"—Hank Williams
3. "Don't Rob Another Man's Castle"—Eddy Arnold
4. "Candy Kisses"—George Morgan
5. "Wedding Bells"—Hank Williams

1950   Hank Snow joins the Grand Ole Opry.

TOP RECORDS:
1. "I'm Movin' On"—Hank Snow
2. "Chattanoogie Shoe Shine Boy"—Red Foley
3. "Why Don't You Love Me?"—Hank Williams
4. "Long Gone Lonesome Blues"—Hank Williams
5. "Shotgun Boogie"—Tennessee Ernie Ford

1951   The trend begun by Bing Crosby continues: Pop singers continue to have hits with country material, especially Patti Page with "Tennessee Waltz" and Tony Bennett with "Cold Cold Heart."

TOP RECORDS:
1. "Slowpoke"—Pee Wee King
2. "Always Late"—Lefty Frizzell
3. "Cold Cold Heart"—Hank Williams
4. "Rhumba Boogie"—Hank Snow
5. "Let Old Mother Nature Have Her Way"—Carl Smith

1952   Hank Williams leaves the Grand Ole Opry.

Tex Ritter sings the theme song in *High Noon* and wins an Academy Award the following year for best song in a motion picture.

Eddy Arnold is Perry Como's summer replacement on NBC-TV.

Deaths of Uncle Dave Macon, Rabon Delmore, and super-promoter J. L. Frank.

Kitty Wells, Johnny and Jack, Webb Pierce, Faron Young, and Ray Price join the Grand Ole Opry.

TOP RECORDS:
1. "Wild Side of Life"—Hank Thompson
2. "Jambalaya"—Hank Williams
3. "I Didn't Know God Made Honky-Tonk Angels"—Kitty Wells
4. "Don't Just Stand There"—Carl Smith
5. "Indian Love Call"—Slim Whitman

1953   Death of Hank Williams on New Year's Day.

The Jimmy Dean show begins telecasting on CBS network television..

"Town Hall Party" goes on television in California.

Jim Reeves joins the Louisiana Hayride.

TOP RECORDS:
1. "There Stands the Glass"—Webb Pierce
2. "Kaw-Liga"—Hank Williams
3. "Dear John Letter"—Jean Shepard and Ferlin Husky
4. "I Forgot More Than You'll Ever Know about Him"—Davis Sisters
5. "It's Been So Long"—Webb Pierce

1954   Beginnings of rockabilly: Bill Haley changes the name of his band from the Saddle Pals to the Comets; records "Rock Around the Clock." Elvis cuts his first records for Sun in Memphis.

Webb Pierce's "Slowly" features the pedal steel guitar (played by Bud Isaacs) for the first time.

Death of Fred Rose.

TOP RECORDS:
1. "I Don't Hurt Any More"—Hank Snow
2. "Slowly"—Webb Pierce

    3. "More and More"—Webb Pierce
    4. "Loose Talk"—Carl Smith
    5. "One by One"—Kitty Wells and Red Foley

1955   Johnny Cash first records for Sun Records.

Flatt and Scruggs, the Louvin Brothers, Jim Reeves, Hawkshaw Hawkins join the Grand Ole Opry.

George Jones has his first hit: "Why Baby Why?"

TOP RECORDS:
1. "In the Jailhouse Now"—Webb Pierce
2. "I Don't Care/Your Good for Nothing Heart"—Webb Pierce
3. "Sixteen Tons"—Tennessee Ernie Ford
4. "Love Love Love"—Webb Pierce
5. "Mystery Train"—Elvis Presley

1956   Chet Atkins hired by RCA as manager of their studios on Nashville's 17th Avenue South.

Eddy Arnold does a network television show on ABC.

George D. Hay retires from the Grand Ole Opry.

Billboard changes their country listings to "C&W."

TOP RECORDS:
1. "Heartbreak Hotel"—Elvis Presley
2. "Singing the Blues"—Marty Robbins
3. "Crazy Arms"—Ray Price
4. "Don't Be Cruel"/"Hound Dog"—Elvis Presley
5. "I Walk the Line"—Johnny Cash

1957   A rash of rockabilly: country rockers go pop with "Bye Bye Love," "Young Love," "A White Sport Coat," "Whole Lotta Shakin' Going On."

The Everly Brothers are signed as a country act and join the Grand Ole Opry.

Rise of urban interest in bluegrass and old time music: the Country Gentlemen form in Washington D.C. and the New Lost City Ramblers form in New York City.

Patsy Cline wins Arthur Godfrey's Talent Scouts, sings "Walkin' after Midnight," which is also her first hit.

The foundation of the powerful and influential trade organization, the Country Music Association.

TOP RECORDS:
1. "Fraulein"—Bobby Helms
2. "(Since You've) Gone"—Ferlin Husky
3. "Bye Bye Love"/"Wake Up Little Suzie"—Everly Brothers
4. "Young Love"—Sonny James
5. "White Sport Coat"—Marty Robbins

1958   BMI opens a Nashville office.

"Tom Dooley" wins the first country music Grammy Award; the start of the folk boom, which will introduce thousands to country music.

Elvis is drafted.

Stereo records are introduced.

TOP RECORDS:
1. "City Lights"/"Invitation to the Blues"—Ray Price
2. "Oh Lonesome Me"/"I Can't Stop Loving You"—Don Gibson
3. "Guess Things Happen That Way"—Johnny Cash

4. "Big River"/"Ballad of a Teenage Queen"—Johnny Cash
5. "Send Me the Pillow You Dream on"—Hank Locklin

1959   Buck Owens begins hit recording career with first major hit, "Under Your Spell Again," he goes against popular trend by not moving to Nashville but instead begins to build Bakersfield, California, as a recording and music center.

Historical epic songs are in vogue.

TOP RECORDS:
1. "The Battle of New Orleans"—Johnny Horton
2. "He'll Have to Go"—Jim Reeves
3. "El Paso"—Marty Robbins
4. "The Three Bells"—The Browns
5. "Heartaches By the Number"—Ray Price

1960   WLS drops the National Barn Dance; the show, with many of the old regular cast, moves to WGN in Chicago for another decade.

Jimmie Davis elected to a second term as governor of Louisiana.

Porter Wagoner starts his syndicated televison show, which is still running.

TOP RECORDS:
1. "Please Help Me I'm Falling"—Hank Locklin
2. "Alabam"—Cowboy Copas
3. "On the Wings of a Dove"—Ferlin Husky
4. "North to Alaska"—Johnny Horton
5. "Above and Beyond"—Buck Owens

1961   The first country music encyclopedia published: Linnell Gentry's *A History and Encyclopedia of Country, Western, and Gospel Music.*

The first election to the Country Music Hall of Fame. The initial members: Jimmie Rodgers, Fred Rose, and Hank Williams

TOP RECORDS:
1. "Walk on By"—LeRoy Van Dyke
2. "Don't Worry"—Marty Robbins
3. "Hello Walls"—Faron Young
4. "I Fall to Pieces"—Patsy Cline
5. "Big Bad John"—Jimmy Dean

1962   The John Edwards Memorial Foundation, country music's first research center, is incorporated at UCLA.

Loretta Lynn's first hit record: "Success."

Roy Acuff elected to the Country Music Hall of Fame, becoming the first living member.

Music for television's "Beverly Hillbillies" written and performed by Flatt and Scruggs.

TOP RECORDS:
1. "Don't Let Me Cross over"—Carl Butler and Pearl
2. "Wolverton Mountain"—Claude King
3. "Devil Woman"—Marty Robbins
4. "Mama Sang a Song"—Bill Anderson
5. "She Thinks I Still Care"—George Jones

1963   ASCAP opens a Nashville office.

Red Sovine urges a young singer named Charley Pride to move to Nashville from Great Falls, Montana.

The year of tragic death in country music: Patsy Cline, Hawkshaw Hawkins, Cowboy Copas, and Randy Hughes killed in a plane crash; Jack Anglin killed in an automobile accident; Texas Ruby killed in a fire in her house trailer.

"Detroit City," the anthem for the disposessed, released.

Billboard renames their country charts "Hot Country Singles."

TOP RECORDS:
1. "Love's Gonna Live Here"—Buck Owens
2. "Still"—Bill Anderson
3. "Ring of Fire"—Johnny Cash
4. "Act Naturally"—Buck Owens
5. "Lonesome 7-7203"—Hawkshaw Hawkins

1964   SESAC opens a Nashville office.

Dolly Parton graduates from Sevier County High School, moves to Nashville to find fame and fortune.

Tex Ritter elected to the Country Music Hall of Fame.

Jimmy Dean goes on ABC network television.

Johnny Cash brings commercial folk and country together when he records Bob Dylan's "It Ain't Me, Babe."

Your Cheatin' Heart, a film based on the life of Hank Williams and starring George Hamilton as Williams, is released.

TOP RECORDS:
1. "Once a Day"—Connie Smith
2. "Dang Me"—Roger Miller
3. "My Heart Skips a Beat"—Buck Owens
4. "I Guess I'm Crazy"—Jim Reeves
5. "I Don't Care"—Buck Owens

1965   Former Rhodes Scholar Kris Kristofferson moves to Nashville.

Tex Ritter joins the Grand Ole Opry.

The Academy of Country and Western Music (now the Academy of Country Music) formed on the west coast.

Roger Miller dominates the Grammy Awards, winning six awards, unequalled before or since.

Ernest Tubb elected to the Country Music Hall of Fame.

First bluegrass festival is held near Fincastle, Virginia.

TOP RECORDS:
1. "King of the Road"—Roger Miller
2. "Flowers on the Wall"—Statler Brothers
3. "Giddyup Go"—Red Sovine
4. "I've Got a Tiger by the Tail"—Buck Owens
5. "Make the World Go Away"—Eddy Arnold

1966   The first major book-length publication on country music published: Shelton and Goldblatt's *A Picture History of Country and Western Music*.

Uncle Dave Macon, George D. Hay, Eddy Arnold, and Jim Denny elected to the Country Music Hall of Fame.

"Roger Miller Show" aired on NBC-TV.

First issue of *Bluegrass Unlimited* is published.

TOP RECORDS:
1. "Almost Persuaded"—David Houston
2. "There Goes My Everything"—Jack Greene
3. "Think of Me"—Buck Owens
4. "Waitin' in Your Welfare Line"—Buck Owens
5. "Distant Drums"—Jim Reeves

1967   The first time one billion dollars in record sales is achieved.

The Country Music Association begins their annual award show.

Tammy Wynette begins recording.

Red Foley, Jim Reeves, J. L. Frank, and Steve Sholes elected to the Country Music Hall of Fame.

The Country Music Hall of Fame opens.

Top Records:
1. "All the Time"—Jack Greene
2. "Where Does the Good Times Go"—Buck Owens
3. "Sam's Place"—Buck Owens
4. "I Don't Wanna Play House"—Tammy Wynette
5. "It's the Little Things"—Sonny James

1968   Glen Campbell has summer replacement series for the Smothers Brothers.

"Foggy Mountain Breakdown" used as theme music in the film *Bonnie and Clyde.*

A year of many deaths: Red Foley, George D. Hay, Ernest "Pop" Stoneman, Steve Sholes, Clarence Ashley, Dorsey Dixon, Luther Perkins, and Bill Cox.

Chet Atkins promoted to vice president of RCA Records.

Bob Wills elected to the Country Music Hall of Fame.

John Lair sells Renfro Valley.

Top Records:
1. "Harper Valley P.T.A."—Jeannie C. Riley
2. "Stand By Your Man"—Tammy Wynette
3. "Folsom Prison Blues"—Johnny Cash
4. "D-I-V-O-R-C-E"—Tammy Wynette
5. "Skip a Rope"—Henson Cargill

1969   Country Music comes to television in a big way: "The Glen Campbell Goodtime Hour" and "Hee Haw" on CBS; "The Johnny Cash Show" on ABC.

Flatt and Scruggs split, each forming his own band.

Bob Dylan records his "Nashville Skyline" album.

Bill Malone's *Country Music USA* published; the first full-length scholarly look at country music's history.

Groundbreaking for Opryland USA, country-music-oriented amusement park just outside Nashville.

Gene Autry elected to the Country Music Hall of Fame.

Top Records:
1. "A Boy Named Sue"—Johnny Cash
2. "Daddy Sang Bass"—Johnny Cash
3. "Okie from Muskogee"—Merle Haggard
4. "Only the Lonely"—Sonny James
5. "Since I Met You Baby"—Sonny James

1970   Tex Ritter runs for the U.S. Senate from Tennessee.

Bill Monroe, the original Carter Family, elected to the Country Music Hall of Fame.

Former Beatle Ringo Starr cuts an album in Nashville.

Top Records:
1. "For the Good Times"—Ray Price
2. "Rose Garden"—Lynn Anderson
3. "Hello Darlin' "—Conway Twitty

      4. "Don't Keep Me Hangin' On"—Sonny James
      5. "Sunday Morning Coming Down"—Johnny Cash

1971   *Country Music* magazine starts.

      Art Satherley elected to the Country Music Hall of Fame.

      TOP RECORDS:
      1. "Help Me Make It Through the Night"—Sammi Smith
      2. "Easy Loving"—Freddie Hart
      3. "Kiss an Angel Good Morning"—Charley Pride
      4. "Empty Arms"—Sonny James
      5. "I Won't Mention It Again"—Ray Price

1972   Loretta Lynn wins CMA's Entertainer of the Year award, the first woman so honored.

      The Country Music Foundation Library and Media Center formally opens.

      Willie Nelson hosts an Austin-oriented country music festival in Dripping Springs, Texas.

      Opryland USA opens to the public.

      Tom T. Hall hires Johnny Rodriguez as guitarist for his band in May; by the end of the year Rodriguez is a star in his own right with a hit record, "Pass Me By."

      Jimmie Davis elected to the Country Music Hall of Fame.

      TOP RECORDS:
      1. "Happiest Girl in the Whole U.S.A."—Donna Fargo
      2. "My Hangup Is You"—Freddie Hart
      3. "Woman (Sensuous Woman)"—Don Gibson
      4. "Funny Face"—Donna Fargo
      5. "She's Got to Be a Saint"—Ray Price

1973   Continued nationwide interest in country music highlighted by Loretta Lynn featured on the cover of *Newsweek.*

      Chet Atkins and Patsy Cline elected to the Country Music Hall of Fame.

      TOP RECORDS:
      1. "Behind Closed Doors"—Charlie Rich
      2. "Let Me Be There"—Olivia Newton-John
      3. "If We Make It Through December"—Merle Haggard
      4. "Satin Sheets"—Jeannie Pruett
      5. "Why Me"—Kris Kristofferson

1974   George Hamilton IV is the first country singer to appear in the USSR.

      The Grand Ole Opry moves to a new building at Opryland USA.

      Merle Haggard featured on the cover of *Time.*

      The first book-length look at the Austin scene appears: Jan Reid's *The Improbable Rise of Redneck Rock.*

      Pee Wee King and Owen Bradley elected to the Country Music Hall of Fame.

      TOP RECORDS:
      1. "Most Beautiful Girl"—Charlie Rich
      2. "If You Love Me Let Me Know"—Olivia Newton-John
      3. "I Can Help"—Billy Swan
      4. "I Love"—Tom T. Hall
      5. "He Thinks I Still Care"—Anne Murray

1975   Tom T. Hall and Dolly Parton formulate plans for syndicated television shows.

      A year of multiple deaths: Lefty Frizzell, George Morgan, Charlie Monroe, Sam McGee, Clark Kessinger, and Bob Wills; also important industry figures Oscar Davis and Bill Williams.

Minnie Pearl elected to the Country Music Hall of Fame.

Top Records:
1. "Back Home Again"—John Denver
2. "Before the Next Teardrop Falls"—Freddy Fender
3. "I'm Not Lisa"—Jessi Colter
4. "Wasted Days and Wasted Nights"—Freddy Fender
5. "When Will I Be Loved"—Linda Ronstadt

DISCOGRAPHY

Introduction

"A Day in the Mountains—1928" County 512
"A Fiddlers' Convention in Mountain City, Tennessee" County 525
"Anglo-American Ballads" Library of Congress 1
"Come All You Coal Miners" Rounder 4005
"Drones and Chanters: Irish Bagpipes" Claddagh 1
"Early Rural String Bands" RCA Victor LPV-552
Sarah Ogan Gunning, "Sarah Ogan Gunning" Folk-Legacy 26
Tom T. Hall, "In Search of a Song" Mercury SR 61350
"Old Time Southern Dance Music: The String Bands" Old Timey LP101
"Smokey Mountain Ballads" RCA Victor LPV-507
"Star Above the Garter: Irish Fiddle Music" Claddagh 5
"Steel Guitar Classics" Old Timey 113
"Texas-Mexican Border Music" Folk-Lyric 1003
Little Roy Wiggins and Kayton Roberts, "Twin Steel Guitars" Stoneway 129
Chubby Wise, "Chubby Plays Polkas" Stoneway 118

Old Time Music

Roy Acuff, "All Time Greatest Hits," Hickory LPS 109
_____, "Roy Acuff's Greatest Hits," Columbia CS 1034
Bob Atcher, "Dean of the Cowboy Singers," Columbia CL-2232
Bailey Brothers, "Take Me Back to Happy Valley," Rounder 0030
Blue Sky Boys, "The Blue Sky Boys (Bill and Earl Bolick)," Bluebird AXM2-5525
Dwight Butcher, "Dwight Butcher, 1933-1934," Certified CTF 1502
Fiddlin' John Carson, "The Old Hen Cackled and the Rooster's Going to Crow," Rounder 1003
Carter Family, "The Carter Family on Border Radio," JEMF 101
_____, " 'Mid the Green Fields of Virginia," RCA LPM 2772
_____, "The Original and Great Carter Family," Camden CAL-586
Wilma Lee and Stoney Cooper, "Family Favorites," Hickory LPM 106
Delmore Brothers, "The Delmore Brothers," Bluebird (forthcoming)
Curly Fox, "Curly Fox," vols. 1-2, Rural Rhythm 251, 252
Girls of the Golden West, "Girls of the Golden West," Bluebonnet 106
Tom T. Hall, "I Witness Life," Mercury 61277

DISCOGRAPHY

Grayson and Whitter, "The Recordings of Grayson and Whitter," County 513
Johnny and Jack, "The Best of Johnny and Jack," RCA VPM-6022
Bradley Kincaid, "Bradley Kincaid," vols. 1-3, Bluebonnet 107, 112, 118
Louvin Brothers, "Tragic Songs of Life," Capitol T-769
Mac and Bob (McFarland and Gardner), "Mac and Bob," Birch 1944
Uncle Dave Macon, "The Dixie Dewdrop," Vetco LP-101
_____, "Uncle Dave Macon Volume 2," Vetco LP-102
J. E. Mainer's Mountaineers, "J. E. Mainer's Mountaineers," Arhoolie 5002
Wade Mainer, "Wade Mainer and the Sons of the Mountaineers," County 404
Sam McGee, "Sam McGee," Arhoolie 5012
Sam and Kirk McGee and Arthur Smith, "Old Timers of the Grand Ole Opry," Folkways 2379
Red River Dave McEnery, "Red River Dave," Bluebonnet BL 119
New Lost City Ramblers, "Depression Songs," Folkways 5264
_____, "Remembrance of Things to Come," Folkways 2432
Molly O'Day, "The Heart and Soul of Molly," Mastertone 80313
_____, "Molly O'Day," Old Homestead CS 101
Charlie Poole, "Charlie Poole and the North Carolina Ramblers," vols. 1-3, County 505, 509, 516
The Skillet Lickers, "The Skillet Lickers," vols. 1-2, County 506, 526
Ernest Stoneman, "Ernest V. Stoneman and His Dixie Mountaineers, 1927-1928," Historical HLP 8004
Lulu Belle and Scotty (Wiseman), "Lulu Belle and Scotty," Starday 206
Various, "A Treasury of Immortal Performances," RCA LVB-2094-5
_____, "Echoes of the Ozarks," vols. 1-3, County 518-520
_____, "Grand Ole Opry Pioneer Stars, 1925-1942," Bluebird (forthcoming)
_____, "Opry Old Timers," Starday SLP-182

The Blues

Gene Autry, "Gene Autry—The Victor Recordings 1931-1933," Bluebird (forthcoming)
Cliff Carlisle, "Cliff Carlisle," vols. 1-2, Old Timey, 103, 104
Darby and Tarleton, "Darby and Tarleton," Old Timey 112
Merle Haggard, "Same Train, a Different Time," Capitol SWBB 223
Riley Puckett, "Riley Puckett," GHP LP 902
Jimmie Rodgers, "Country Music Hall of Fame," RCA Victor LPM 2531
_____, "Jimmie the Kid," RCA Victor LPM 2213
_____, "My Rough and Rowdy Ways," RCA Victor LPM 2112
"Negro Blues and Field Hollers," Library of Congress 59

Comedy

Don Bowman, "Recorded Almost Live," RCA LPM 3646
Jerry Clower, "Mouth of the Mississippi," MCA MCA 47
_____, "Yazoo, Mississippi, Talkin'," MCA MCA 33
Homer and Jethro, "The Far-Out World of Homer and Jethro," RCA LSP 4646
_____, "The Humorous Side of Country Music," Camden CAS 768
Grandpa Jones, "Everybody's Grandpa," Monument MLP 8083
Grandpa Jones and Minnie Pearl, "Grand Ole Opry Stars—Grandpa Jones and Minnie Pearl," RCA ADL2-0701
Lonzo and Oscar, "Country Comedy Time," Decca DL 4363
Minnie Pearl, "America's Beloved Minnie Pearl," Starday SLP 380
Stringbean, "Me and My Old Crow," Nugget NRLP 102
Gid Tanner and his Skillet Lickers, "A Corn Likker Still in Georgia," Voyager VRLP 303

Singing Cowboys

Jules Verne Allen, "The Texas Cowboy," Folk Variety 12502
Rex Allen, "Golden Songs of the Golden West," Vocalion S73885

Gene Autry, "Gene Autry's Country Music Hall of Fame," Columbia CS 1035
_____, "Gene Autry's Greatest Hits," Columbia CL 1575
Johnny Bond, "Johnny Bond's Best," Harmony HL 7308
_____, "How I Love Them Old Songs," Lamb and Lion LLC 4002
Wilf Carter (Montana Slim), "Wilf Carter," vols. 1-2, CMH 111, 120
Eddie Dean, "Sincerely, Eddie Dean," Shasta LP 513
Tex Ritter, "An American Legend," Capitol SKC 11241
_____, "Tex Ritter's Wild West," Capitol ST 2914
Roy Rogers, "The Best of Roy Rogers," Camden ACL1-0953(e)
Marty Robbins, "Gunfighter Ballads and Trail Songs," Columbia CS 8158
Sons of the Pioneers, "Riders in the Sky," Camden ADL2-0336(e)
_____, "Sons of the Pioneers," JEMF 102
Carl T. Sprague, "The First Popular Singing Cowboy," Folk Variety 12502
Jimmy Wakely, "Santa Fe Trail," Decca DL 8409
Foy Willing and the Riders of the Purple Sage, "Cowboy," Roulette R-25035
Various, "Authentic Cowboys and Their Western Folksongs," RCA LPV-522
_____, "The Cowboy, His Songs, Ballads, and Brag Talk," Folkways FH 5723
_____, "Cowboy Songs and Ballads," Library of Congress 28

Cajun

Balfa Brothers, "The Balfa Brothers," Swallow 6019
Boisec, "Creole Cajun Blues," Arhoolie 1070
Clifton Chenier, "King of the Bayous," Arhoolie 1052
Hackberry Ramblers, "Hackberry Ramblers," Arhoolie 5003
Doug Kershaw, "Cajun Way," Warner Brothers 5-1820
Jimmy C. Newman, "Folk Songs of the Bayou Country," Decca DL 4398
_____, "Lache Pas La Patate," La Louisianne 140
Louisiana Aces, "The Louisiana Aces," Rounder 6003
Ambrose Thibodeaux, "Ambrose Thibodeaux," La Louisianne 112
_____, "The Cajun Country Fiddle," La Louisianne 129
Various, "Allons Au Fais Do-Do," Swallow 6009
_____, "Cajun Music of the Early '50s," Arhoolie 5008
_____, "Folksongs of the Louisiana Acadians," Arhoolie 5009
_____, "Louisiana Cajun Music," vols. 1-5, Old Timey 108-111, 114

Bluegrass

Hylo Brown/The Lonesome Pine Fiddlers, "Hylo Brown Meets the Lonesome Pine Fiddlers," Starday
    SDK 220
Country Gentlemen, "Best of the Early Country Gentlemen," Rebel 1492
_____, "Yesterday and Today," vols. 1-3, Rebel 1521, 1527, 1535
Lester Flatt and Earl Scruggs, "Country Music," Mercury MG 20358
Jim and Jesse, "Superior Sounds of Bluegrass," Old Dominion ODM 02
Jimmy Martin, "Good 'N' Country," MCA-81
Monroe Brothers, "Feast Here Tonight," Bluebird AXM2-5510
Bill Monroe, "Bean Blossom," MCA MCA2-8002
_____, "The High Lonesome Sound," Decca DL 4780
Charlie Monroe, "Charlie Monroe on the Noonday Jamboree—1944," County 538
Clyde Moody, "Moody's Blues," Old Homestead 90013
The Seldom Scene, "Act I-III," Rebel 1511, 1520, 1528
Reno and Harrell, "Bicentennial Bluegrass," Monument
Don Reno, "Fastest Five String Alive," King SDK 1065
Stanley Brothers, "Early Classics," Melodeon 7322
_____, "The Stanley Brothers in Person," King SDK 719
Mac Wiseman, " 'Tis Sweet to Be Remembered," Dot DLP 25084
Osborne Brothers, "The Osborne Brothers Bobby and Sonny," MCA MCA DL 5356

DISCOGRAPHY

Western Swing

Asleep at the Wheel, "Asleep at the Wheel," Epic KE 33097
———, "Texas Gold," Capitol ST 114411
Bill Boyd, "Bill Boyd's Cowboy Ramblers," Bluebird AXM2-5503
Spade Cooley, "Fidoodlin'," Republic RLP 1302
Merle Haggard, "A Tribute to the Best Damn Fiddler in the World (or, My Salute to Bob Wills),"
    Capitol ST 638
Laura Lee, "Everything Changes But Laura Lee," Footprint FPS 1001
Leon McAuliffe, "Mr. Western Swing," Pine Mountain 271
———, "Take It Away, Leon," Stoneway 139
Hank Thompson, "Twenty-Fifth Anniversary Album," Dot DOS2–2000
Bob Wills, "Bob Wills Anthology," Columbia KG 32416
———, "For The Last Time," United Artists LA-216 (J2) 0098
———, "The Legendary Bob Wills," Columbia P212922
Various, "Beer Parlor Jive," String 801
———, "Western Swing," OldTimey 105

Gospel

Blackwood Brothers, "Gospel Classics by the Blackwood Brothers," RCA LSP-4279
Martha Carson, "A Talk with the Lord," Capitol T-1607
Johnny Cash, "World's Greatest Hymns," Columbia C-32246
Chuck Wagon Gang, "Revival Time," Columbia CS-9673
———, "That Old Time Religion," Columbia CS-9018
Jimmie Davis, "Singing the Gospel," MCA MCA-118
Florida Boys Quartet, "Florida Boys in Nashville," Canaan 9601
Stuart Hamblen, "Cowboy Church," Word 8504
Happy Goodman Family, "It's a Wonderful Feeling," Canaan 9617
LeFevre Family, "Fifty Golden Years," Canaan 9694
Lewis Family, "Come Sunday," Canaan 9753
Louvin Brothers, "The Great Gospel Songs of the Louvin Brothers," Capitol ST 11193
Oak Ridge Boys, "New Horizons," Heartwarming 1988
———, "Oak Ridge Boys," Columbia KC-32742
Singing Rambos, "Singing Rambos . . . Live!," Heartwarming 3116
Connie Smith, "Good Old Country Gospel," RCA LSP-4778
Speer Family, "In Concert," Heartwarming 3180
Stamps Quartet, "The Touch of His Hand," Heartwarming 3133
J. D. Sumner and the Stamps Quartet, "Something Special," Heartwarming 3181
Porter Wagoner and the Blackwood Brothers Quartet, "The Grand Ole Gospel," RCA LSP-3488
Various, "Family Gospel Album," Starday 370
———, "Sacred Harp Singing," Library of Congress 11

Rockabilly/Country Folk/Country Rock/Underground

Bobby Bare, "Sing Lullabies, Legends, and Lies," RCA CLP2-0290
Richard Betts, "Highway Call," Capricorn 0123
Johnny Cash, "Original Golden Hits," vols. 1-2, Sun International 100, 101
Charlie Daniels Band, "Fire on the Mountain," Kama Sutra 2060
Everly Brothers, "Golden Hits of the Everly Brothers," Warner Brothers 1471
Bill Haley and the Comets, "Golden Hits," MCA MCA2-4010
George Hamilton IV, "Greatest Hits," RCA APL-0455
John Hartford, "Aero-Plain," Warner Brothers 1916
Hot Mud Family, "The Hot Mud Family," Vetco 501
Waylon Jennings, "Ladies Love Outlaws," RCA LSP-4751
Jerry Lee Lewis, "Original Golden Hits," vols. 1-3, Sun 102, 103, 128
Marshall Tucker Band, "Where We All Belong," Capricorn 2C-0145

Willie Nelson, "Red Headed Stranger," Columbia KC 33482
Nitty Gritty Dirt Band, "Will the Circle Be Unbroken?," United Artists UA59081
Carl Perkins, "Blue Suede Shoes," Sun 112
_____, "Original Golden Hits," Sun 111
Poco, "The Very Best Of Poco," Epic PEG33537
Elvis Presley, "Golden Records," vol. 1, RCA LSP 1707
_____, "Elvis Country," RCA LSP-3450
Putnam County String Band, "The Putnam County String Band," Rounder 3002,3003
Charlie Rich, "Original Memphis Rock and Roll," Sun 116
_____, "Behind Closed Doors," Epic PEQ-32247
Linda Ronstadt, "Heart Like a Wheel," Capitol ST-11358
Doc Watson, "Memories," United Artists UA-LA423-H2
Various, "Memphis Country," Sun 120

Honky-Tonk/Country Pop/The Nashville Sound

Bill Anderson, "Bill Anderson's Greatest Hits," MCA MCA-13
Lynn Anderson, "Lynn Anderson's Greatest Hits," Columbia KC-31641
Eddy Arnold, "All Time Favorites," RCA LSP-1223
_____, "Cattle Call," RCA LSP-2578
Chet Atkins, "Chet Atkins Now and . . . Then," RCA VPSX-6079
Elton Britt, "The Best of Elton Britt," vol. 1, RCA LSP 4822
The Browns, "The Best of the Browns," RCA ANL1-1083
Jim Ed Brown, "The Best of Jim Ed Brown," RCA APL1-0324
Jimmy Buffett, "Rancho Deluxe," United Artists UA-LA-466-G
Glen Campbell, "Glen Campbell's Greatest Hits," Capitol SW-752
Johnny Cash, "Live at Folsom Prison," Columbia CS 9639
Roy Clark, "Roy Clark's Family Album," Dot DOS-26018
Patsy Cline, "Patsy Cline's Greatest Hits," MCA MCA-12
Cowboy Copas, "The Best of Cowboy Copas," Starday SLP-458
Floyd Cramer, "The Best of Floyd Cramer," RCA LSP-2888
Skeeter Davis, "The Best of Skeeter Davis," RCA LSP-3374
Jimmy Dean, "Jimmy Dean's Greatest Hits," Columbia CS-9285
John Denver, "An Evening with John Denver," RCA CPL2-0764
Jimmy Dickens, "Jimmy Dickens Greatest Hits," Decca DL 75133
Bob Dylan, "Nashville Skyline," Columbia KCS 9825
Dave Dudley, "The Best of Dave Dudley," Mercury SR 61268
Eagles, "One of These Nights," Asylum 7E-1039
Barbara Fairchild, "Teddy Bear Song," Columbia KC-31720
Freddy Fender, "Before the Next Teardrop Falls," ABC-Dot DOSD-2020
Flying Burrito Brothers, "Flying Again," Columbia PL-33817
Red Foley, "The Red Foley Story," MCA MCA2-4053
Tennessee Ernie Ford, "Sixteen Tons," Capitol DT 1380
Lefty Frizzell, "Lefty Frizzell's Greatest Hits," Columbia CS 9288
Don Gibson, "The Very Best of Don Gibson," Hickory HR 4502
Jack Greene and Jeannie Seeley, "Jack Greene and Jeannie Seeley," MCA MCA-288
Merle Haggard, "The Best of Merle Haggard," Capitol SKAO-2951
Tom T. Hall, "Tom T. Hall's Greatest Hits," Mercury SR-61369
Freddie Hart, "Freddie Hart's Greatest Hits," MCA MCA-67
Emmylou Harris, "Pieces of the Sky," Reprise MS 2213
Johnny Horton, "Johnny Horton's Greatest Hits," Columbia CL 8396
David Houston, "David Houston's Greatest Hits," Columbia BN 26342
Ferlin Husky, "The Best of Ferlin Husky," Capitol SKAO-143
Stonewall Jackson, "The Great Old Songs," Columbia CS 9708
Sonny James, "Young Love," Capitol ST-11196
George Jones, "The Best of George Jones," RCA APL1-0316
_____, "A Picture of Me Without You," Epic KE 31718

DISCOGRAPHY

Kris Kristofferson, "Break Away," Monument PZ-33278
Hank Locklin, "The Best of Hank Locklin," RCA LSP 3559
Loretta Lynn, "Coal Miner's Daughter," MCA 10
_____, "Loretta Lynn's Greatest Hits," MCA 1
Barbara Mandrell, "The Midnight Oil," Columbia KC 32743
Charlie McCoy, "Charlie My Boy," Monument K2-33384
George Morgan, "Remembering: Greatest Hits of George Morgan," Columbia KC 33894
Anne Murray, "Country," Capitol ST-11324
Rick Nelson, "Country," MCA2-4004
New Riders of the Purple Sage, "New Riders of the Purple Sage," Columbia PC-30888
Olivia Newton-John, "Clearly Love," MCA 2148
Buck Owens, "The Best of Buck Owens," vols. 1-5, Capitol ST-2105, ST-2897, SKAO-145, ST-830, and ST-11273
Dolly Parton, "The Best of Dolly Parton," RCA SLP-4999
_____, "My Blue Ridge Mountain Boy," RCA APL1-0033
Dolly Parton and Porter Wagoner, "The Best of Dolly Parton and Porter Wagoner," RCA SLP-4556
Webb Pierce, "Best of Webb Pierce," MCA2-4089
_____, "Greatest Hits," MCA 120
Ray Price, "All Time Greatest Hits," Columbia KE 31364
_____, "Danny Boy," Columbia CS 9477
Charley Pride, "The Best of Charley Pride," RCA LSP-4223
Jerry Reed, "A Good Woman's Love," RCA APL1-0544
Jim Reeves, "Am I That Easy to Forget?," RCA APL1-0039
Marty Robbins, "All Time Greatest Hits," Columbia KG 31361
Jean Shepard, "Slippin' Away," UA-LA144F
Carl Smith, "The Way I Lose My Mind," Hickory H3G-4518
Connie Smith, "The Best of Connie Smith," RCA SLP 3848
Hank Snow, "The Best of Hank Snow," RCA LSP-3478
_____, "This Is My Story," RCA LSP-3478
Mel Tillis, "Live at Houston Coliseum," MGM–4788
Floyd Tillman, "Portrait of Floyd Tillman," Bagatelle LP–92
Merle Travis, "The Best of Merle Travis," Capitol SM-2662
Ernest Tubb, "Ernest Tubb's Greatest Hits," MCA-16
_____, "The Ernest Tubb Story," MCA2-4040
Tanya Tucker, "Tanya Tucker's Greatest Hits," Columbia KC 33355
Conway Twitty, "Look into My Teardrops," MCA-112
T. Texas Tyler, "The Hits of T. Texas Tyler," Capitol ST-2344
Porter Wagoner, "The Carroll County Accident," RCA LSP-4116
Dottie West, "The Best of Dottie West," RCA LSP-4811
Kitty Wells, "Kitty Wells Greatest Hits," MCA-121
_____, "The Kitty Wells Story," MCA2-4031
Slim Whitman, "The Very Best of Slim Whitman," United Artists UA-LA386-E
Don Williams, "Don Williams Greatest Hits," ABC-Dot DOSD-2035
Hank Williams, "24 of Hank Williams Greatest Hits," MGM SE-4755
_____, "The Very Best of Hank Williams," vols 1-2, MGM E-4168, E-4227
Tammy Wynette, "Tammy Wynette's Greatest Hits," Columbia BN-26486
Faron Young, "The Best of Faron Young," Mercury SR-61267
Various, "Chet, Floyd, and Boots," Camden 2523
_____, "Country Hits of the 1940s," Capitol SM-884
_____, "Country Hits of the 1950s," Capitol SM–885
_____, "Country Hits of the 1960s," Capitol SM-886

BIBLIOGRAPHY

GENERAL

Evans, James. *Prairie Farmer and W.L.S.: The Burridge D. Butler Years*. Urbana: University of Illinois Press, 1969.

Gelatt, Roland. *The Fabulous Phonograph*. New York: Appleton-Century, 1966.

Gentry, Linnell. *A History and Encyclopedia of Country, Western, and Gospel Music*. Nashville: Clairmont Press, 1969.

Green, Archie. *Only a Miner: Studies in Recorded Coal Mining Songs*. Urbana: University of Illinois Press, 1972.

Hatcher, Danny, ed. *Proceedings of the 1890 Convention of Local Phonograph Companies*. Nashville: Country Music Foundation Press, 1974.

Horstman, Dorothy. *Sing Your Heart Out, Country Boy*. New York: G. P. Dutton and Company, 1975.

Kinkle, Roger D. *The Complete Encyclopedia of Popular Music and Jazz, 1900-1950*. New Rochelle: Arlington House, 1975.

Malone, Bill C. *Country Music U.S.A.: A Fifty-Year History*. Austin: University of Texas Press, 1968.

Malone, Bill C., and McCulloh, Judith, eds. *Stars of Country Music*. Urbana: University of Illinois Press, 1975.

Price, Steven. *Take Me Home: The Rise of Country and Western Music*. New York: Praeger Publications, 1974.

Read, Oliver; and Welch, Walter L. *From Tin Foil to Stereo: The Evolution of the Phonograph*. New York: Bobbs-Merrill, 1959.

Roberts, Leonard. *Sang Branch Settlers*. Austin: University of Texas Press, 1974.

Shelton, Robert, and Goldblatt, Burt. *The Country Music Story*. New York: Bobbs-Merrill, 1966.

BIBLIOGRAPHY

Shestack, Melvin. *The Country Music Encyclopedia.* New York: Crowell, 1975.

Stambler, Irwin, and Landon, Grelun. *Encyclopedia of Folk, Country, and Western Music.* New York: St. Martin's Press, 1969.

_____. *Golden Guitars.* New York: Four Winds Press, 1971.

OLD-TIME MUSIC

Cohen, Norman, Earle, Eugene W., and Wickham, Graham. *The Early Recording Career of Ernest V. "Pop" Stoneman.* John Edwards Memorial Foundation Special Series number one.

Cohen, John, and Seeger, Mike. *The New Lost City Ramblers Song Book.* New York: Oak Publications, 1964.

Delmore, Alton. *Truth Is Stranger Than Publicity; Alton Delmore's Autobiography.* Nashville: Country Music Foundation Press, 1976.

Laws, Malcolm. *American Balladry from British Broadsides.* Philadelphia: American Folklore Society, 1957.

Orgill, Michael. *Anchored in Love: The Carter Family Story.* Old Tappan, New Jersey: Fleming H. Revell, 1975.

Rinzler, Ralph. *Uncle Dave Macon: A Bio-Discography.* John Edwards Memorial Foundation Special Series number three.

Tribe, Ivan M., and Morris, John W. *Molly O'Day, Lynn Davis, and the Cumberland Mountain Folks.* John Edwards Memorial Foundation Special Series number seven.

Wolfe, Charles K. *The Grand Ole Opry: The Early Years, 1925–35.* London: Old Time Music, 1975.

BLUES

Rodgers, Carrie. *My Husband Jimmie Rodgers.* Nashville: Country Music Foundation Press, 1975.

Russell, Tony. *Blacks, Whites, and Blues.* New York: Stein and Day, 1970.

SINGING COWBOYS

Fife, Austin E. and Alta S. *Cowboy and Western Songs.* New York: Clarkson N. Potter, 1969.

Griffis, Ken. *Hear My Song: The Story of the Celebrated Sons of the Pioneers.* Los Angeles: John Edwards Memorial Foundation, 1974.

CAJUN

Daigle, Pierre. *Tears, Love, and Laughter: The Story of the Acadians.* Church Point, Louisiana: Acadian Publishing Enterprise, 1972.

Post, Lauren C. *Cajun Sketches.* Baton Rouge: Louisiana State University Press, 1974.

Whitfield, Irene. *Louisiana French Folk Songs.* New York: Dover Publications, 1969.

BLUEGRASS

Artis, Bob. *Bluegrass.* New York: Hawthorn Books, 1975.

Price, Steven D. *Old as the Hills.* New York: Viking Press, 1974.

Rooney, Jim. *Bossmen: Bill Monroe and Muddy Waters.* New York: Dial Press, 1971.

Rosenberg, Neil. *Bill Monroe and His Blue Grass Boys: An Illustrated Discography.* Nashville: Country Music Foundation Press, 1974.

WESTERN SWING

Townsend, Charles. *San Antonio Rose: The Life of Bob Wills.* Urbana: University of Illinois Press, 1976.

GOSPEL

Burt, Jesse, and Allen, Duane. *The History of Gospel Music.* Nashville: K & S Press, 1971.

Cash, Johnny. *Man in Black.* Grand Rapids: Zondervan Press, 1975.

Marshall, Howard Wight. *Keep on the Sunny Side of Life: Pattern and Religious Expression in Blue Grass Gospel Music.* John Edwards Memorial Foundation Reprint number 31.

ROCKABILLY, COUNTRY-FOLK, COUNTRY ROCK, AND COUNTRY UNDERGROUND

Escott, Colin, and Hawkins, Martin. *Catalyst: The Sun Records Story.* London: Aquarius Books, 1975.

Reid, Jan. *The Improbable Rise of Redneck Rock.* Austin: Heidelberg Publishers, 1974.

Wren, Christopher. *Winners Got Scars Too: The Life of Johnny Cash.* New York: Dial Press, 1971.

HONKY-TONK, COUNTRY POP, AND THE NASHVILLE SOUND

Atkins, Chet, and Neely, Bill. *Country Gentleman.* Chicago: Henry Regnery, 1974.

Grissim, John. *Country Music: White Man's Blues.* New York: Paperback Library, 1970.

Hemphill, Paul. *The Nashville Sound.* New York: Simon and Schuster, 1970.

Holloran, Carolyn. *Your Favorite Country Music Stars.* New York: Popular Library; 1975.

Lord, Bobby. *Hit the Glory Road.* Nashville: Broadman Press, 1969.

Price, Steven D. *Take Me Home: The Rise of Country and Western Music.* New York: Praeger, 1974.

Williams, Roger. *Sing a Sad Song: The Life of Hank Williams.* New York: Doubleday, 1970.

Wren, Christopher. *Winners Got Scars Too.* New York: Dial Press, 1971.

INDEX